FEEDING HANNIBAL

A CONNOISSEUR'S COOKBOOK

ACKNOWLEDGMENTS

Between the covers of this cookbook rest the efforts of many. I cannot thank them enough but offer my deepest gratitude.

Bryan Fuller, creator and showrunner – whose jaw-dropping creativity and unexpected generosity pushed me beyond the limits of my known universe. Loretta Ramos, co-producer and spirit-guide – who sparked this cookbook project and made it happen with a snap of her tiny but mighty fingers. Beth Lewis, Managing Editor, and her publishing team – who made my experience with Titan Books a pure joy.

Love and grats to sibs: Char and Harv for recipe ideas and Joyce and Al for assisting me with prop and food styling for Brilynn's wonderful photos. Victoria Walsh who went far beyond her food styling duties on *Hannibal* by taking behind-the-scenes photos, getting me going on social media and being so positive always. Alison Fryer of George Brown College and Diane Hargrave of DHPR – whose influence and savvy helped grow this project on multiple platforms. For advice and recommendations, my gratitude to Helen Field, Ettie and Barry Shuken, John Kruusi, Jennifer McLagen and JC William.

Thank you also to Martha De Laurentiis, Tim Farish and Robert Sorkin at Gaumont, Akiva Griffith at NBC, Brian Hirsch at Sony, Kirsti Tichenor and Travis Rutherford at Evolution, my agent, Monica Pacheco at McDermid & Assoc, Mads Mikkelsen and José Andrés.

A very special mention to The Fannibals – those candles in the wind whose unfaltering flames of affection and spirit buoyed my belief in this project long after Hannibal and Will slipped over the cliff of cancellation.

Love and gratitude to my parents - Lady Star and Sir Alfred Stanley.

Food sketches by Janice Poon
Original food photography by Brilynn Ferguson featured on pages 17, 24, 25, 28, 39, 45, 51, 61, 65, 75, 78, 80, 91, 92, 97, 98, 109, 111, 119, 124, 132, 137, 141, 144, 146, 150, 155, 159, 160, 168, 173, 177, 189, 193, 203, 209, 213, 219, 229, 233
Photograph of José Andrés by Ryan Forbes
All other photography by Brooke Palmer

FEEDING HANNIBAL: A CONNOISSEUR'S COOKBOOK
ISBN: 9781783297665

Published by Titan Books
A division of Titan Publishing Group Ltd.
144 Southwark St.
London
SE1 0UP

First edition: October 2016
10 9 8 7 6 5 4 3 2 1

To receive advance information, news, competitions, and exclusive offers online, please sign up for the Titan newsletter on our website: www.titanbooks.com

Did you enjoy this book? We love to hear from our readers. Please e-mail us at: readerfeedback@titanemail.com or write to Reader Feedback at the above address.

FEEDING HANNIBAL

A CONNOISSEUR'S COOKBOOK

JANICE POON

TITAN BOOKS

CONTENTS

FOREWORD 7

AT HOME WITH HANNIBAL 8

The Batterie de Cuisine of Dr Lecter 10

BREAKFAST 16

APPETIZERS 26

MAINS - MEAT 80

MAINS - FISH AND VEGETARIAN 132

SOUPS, SALADS AND SIDE DISHES 156

DESSERTS AND DRINKS 182

ACHIEVING THE HANNIBAL LOOK 204

THE FOOD STYLISTS LOCKER 204

i. Tricks, Tips and Traumas of the Trade
ii. Inside the Mind of Hannibal

HOW TO HANNIBALIZE YOUR TABLE 212

FOREWORD

MADS MIKKELSEN

The very first encounter I had with anyone from the *Hannibal* production in Toronto, was with Janice.

I landed at Pearson International airport, with two big bags, and was told to go straight to "the food stylist", since we had tons of training to do. I had never met a food stylist before, little less any idea of what that might be, so I was very exited to meet someone who apparently dressed up food.

It turned out a food stylist is a Canadian-Asian woman living in a Toronto flat with garlic, pans, and bones hanging in strings from the ceiling, books about food thrown everywhere, and giant bugs stowed in the fridge. For a split second, standing in her kitchen while she was in the attic to pick up some more "items", I convinced myself it was a setup. There was no show called *Hannibal*, no studios, crew or cast, only me standing here ready to get slaughtered and indeed learn about cannibalism the hard way, by ending up on Janice's dining table.

That didn't happen.

Besides being the sweetest person you could ever run across, Janice turned out to be a master teacher, enabling me to fully master the art of chopping things, setting food on fire, flipping eggs in the air and catching them on a knife edge and presenting a human leg as if it was a pork loin decorated with tomatoes cut into tiny roses. But most importantly she was a master chef.

Whilst the actor spends 15 seconds on screen, cheffing around, taking all the credit, Janice and her team would spend days making each dish look splendid and taste fantastic, and that is the thing. Everything Hannibal and his guests guided into their mouths was pure heaven, from the homemade sausages to the ortolans made of marzipan, from the pork loin to the terrine. A scene where Jack Crawford and Hannibal are enjoying foie gras was strangely tricky to get through. I forgot a line so we HAD to do the scene again, eating more foie gras, and oops, Laurence forgot a line…more foie gras. That's the kind of impact Janice's food has on actors. Now that's a food stylist.

With the hope that you will enjoy this book as much as Hannibal and his guests have enjoyed the recipes in real life, I wish you all bon appetite.

AT HOME WITH HANNIBAL

HANNIBAL COOKS: TOOLS AND RULES

THE BATTERIE DE CUISINE OF DR LECTER

The whips, the grinders, the choppers and saws. Strainers, hooks and racks. These are not implements of torture – they are just a small part of the "batterie de cuisine", or cooking equipment, in Hannibal's well-appointed kitchen. Here, in private, he can subdue, tenderize and transform the wildest most uncouth chunk of humanity into a supremely elegant dinner, the hallmark of civility and culture – even as the sub-zero freezers in his basement groan with the remains of the dead.

Luckily, you won't need to visit the gift shop of the Museum of Implements of Torture to pull off the recipes between these covers. A good sauté pan, a lidded pot large enough for braising (the rude are often tough and need to be slow-cooked), a few good knives, a roasting pan, assorted mixing bowls and a few gadgets are all you need. Plus a sharp sense of adventure!

There is an endless array of cooking gadgets available if you want to add more to your kitchen kit. Here are a few pieces of specialized equipment that will help you cook more like a cannibal than a can'tibal.

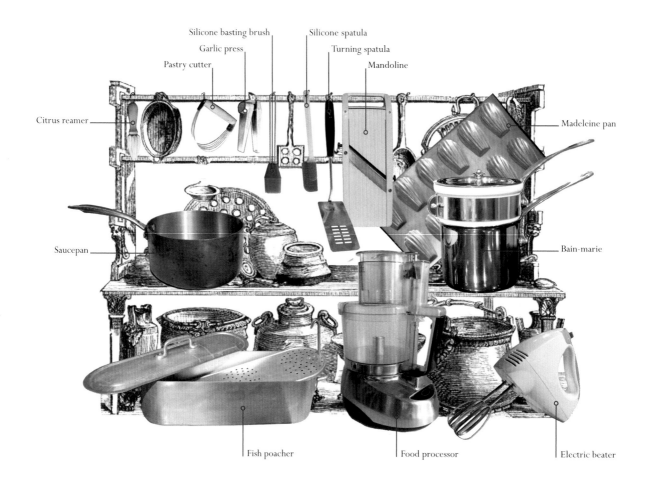

Silicone basting brush · Garlic press · Pastry cutter · Silicone spatula · Turning spatula · Mandoline · Citrus reamer · Madeleine pan · Saucepan · Bain-marie · Fish poacher · Food processor · Electric beater

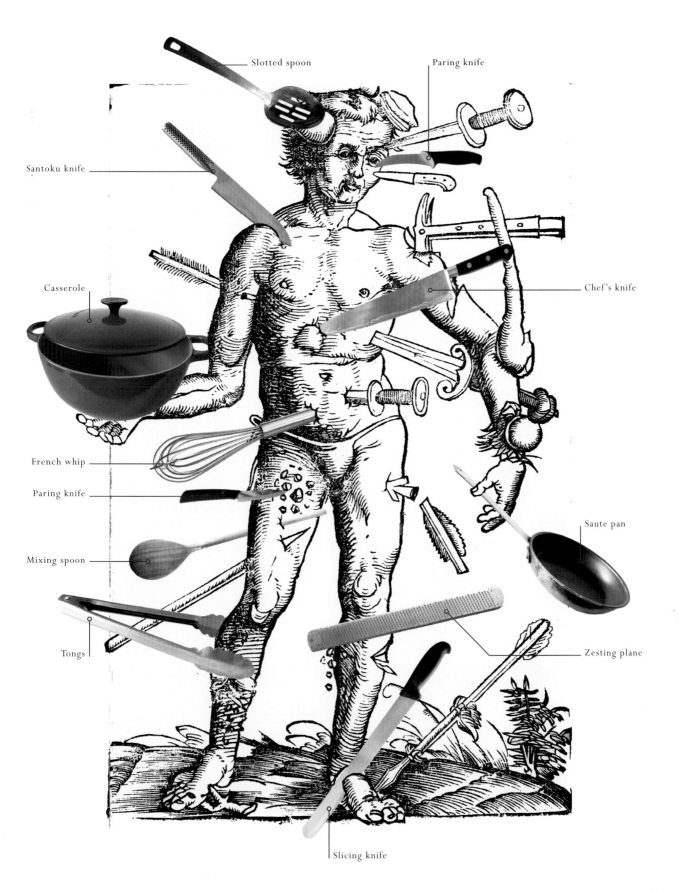

Slotted spoon

Paring knife

Santoku knife

Casserole

Chef's knife

French whip

Paring knife

Mixing spoon

Saute pan

Tongs

Zesting plane

Slicing knife

TECHNIQUES AND TIPS

With a Japanese steel blade flashing on his solid maple chopping block, Hannibal carves his rough quarry into delicate morsels. Then tosses all into his copper sauté pan to sizzle over his six-burner professional gas stove. He tempers the seared flesh with fragrant seasonings, then quells the heat with a splash of fine wine. He serves the dish forth to eager diners – the enticing aromas enveloping them, dispelling any doubts. Master a few of Hannibal's kitchen techniques and your guests, too, will be awed!

Flambé: By flambéing a dish, you add the mellow flavours of scotch, brandy or cognac but not the astringent sting of their alcohol content. Using an 80% proof liquor, measure the amount you wish to use into a heat-proof cup or ladle and warm it. Pour liquor over food in the hot sauté pan, then, if you are cooking on gas, tip the pan slightly so the heat of the flame contacts the fumes of the liquor. As soon as the flame catches, level the pan and shake it gently until the flame subsides. If you are using an electric burner, hold a lighted match just above the liquor until the fumes ignite.

Deglaze: After sautéing ingredients, you will often have browned bits stuck to the bottom of your pan. Deglaze it by adding water, stock or wine to the hot pan. The boiling action and a little scraping with a fork will release these delicious nuggets into the liquid and form the basis of a sauce.

Dredge: To help browning, ingredients are often dredged before sautéing. Don't worry, you will not have to drag the river for bodies, this simply means coated in flour. Just put the flour on a plate or on a board, add crushed herbs if desired, and roll the meat or vegetable in the flour until well-coated.

Rock-chop: When mincing herbs or chopping onions, we long to have great knife-skills. But as every samurai will tell you, it takes practice. Try this technique for dicing up carrots sticks. Using a chef's knife, and keeping the tip of the knife on the board, rock the knife up and down, rotating the blade gradually from right to left across the carrot sticks to dice them for your Osso Buco. Use the same technique for celery sticks and onion slices. It takes a bit of practice, but soon you'll be chopping like a rock star.

Adding Zest: A grating of fresh lemon peel or ginger can add zing to your dishes and drinks. A zest plane makes this easy work – just drag the citrus or root across the plane a few times and it's done!

Basic Stocks and Sauces

One of the simplest best things you can do to improve your home-cooking is to brew your own soup stocks and broths. Substitute them whenever water is called for in a savoury recipe or instead of wine if you don't want to use alcohol.

The basic technique for all stock is the same: for clear light stock, use raw bones; for darker richer stock, brown bones in the oven prior to making stock. Transfer bones/vegetables to a large stock pot, fill with cold water to cover then bring to boil over medium-high heat. Turn heat down to low and simmer for 1-5 hours, depending on type of stock (for beef, pork or lamb, 4-5 hours; for poultry 2-3 hours; for fish and vegetable stocks, see below.)

Skim off and discard any foam that collects at the top and add water as necessary to keep bones/vegetables submerged. Strain, discard bones and taste. If broth is not flavourful enough, boil over high heat to reduce volume until broth tastes rich and delicious. Keep in the freezer in 1 and 2 cup containers (I use zipper baggies) so stock is ready to toss into the pot when you need some.

Fish stock: Use bony off-cuts such as head, collar, bones from filleting. You can get these very inexpensively from your fish market but be sure they are fresh. They should smell faintly of the sea. A stronger "fishy" smell means the fish is old. Add shrimp, crab or lobster shells for a very rich flavour but do not simmer for more than an hour or the stock will turn bitter.

Vegetable stock: Save all your vegetable peelings and trimmings in fridge or freezer, then when you have enough, transfer to a large stock pot, add water and proceed as per basic stock technique. For a very rich flavour, brown several sliced onions in butter then add to vegetable trimmings for stock. Simmer for 1-2 hours.

Bloody Good Sauces

From early history, blood was used to thicken sauces and some of the most elevated dishes still use it: Lièvre à la royale, the ultimate in French cuisine, calls for whole poached hare to be coated in blood sauce. Because cooked blood turns dark brown, this makes it look like a giant chocolate Easter bunny. The best venison stew is thickened not with flour but with the blood of the fallen stag, and Philippino favourite, Dinguan is swimming in black blood.

Hannibal's plates require the more startling look of fresh blood: bright crimson flowing onto his pristine plates like blood gushing from a cut onto newly fallen snow. For that, I recommend Cumberland Sauce (p123) or Aji Pepper Sauce (p88) for roast or grilled meat; Raspberry Coulis (p215) for sweets; and for salads or vegetables, Beet Juice Vinaigrette (p170).

HAVING FRIENDS
FOR DINNER

BREAKFAST

The very first food scene we ever shot with Mads Mikkelsen (Hannibal) and Hugh Dancy (Will), appropriately, was breakfast. After all, on memorable mornings, the best meal of the day is the first one – even if you're a jaded cannibal killer. Especially if you are making a new friend, feeding an old enemy… or feeding an old enemy to a new friend.

PROTEIN SCRAMBLE

The secret to tender creamy eggs is to cook them slowly; high heat will make them rubbery. For juicy sausages, poach them before you brown them. This keeps them plump and boils away excess fat.

INGREDIENTS:

2 honey garlic farm-style breakfast
   sausages
6 eggs
¼ cup heavy cream
butter, oil for sautéeing
salt and pepper to taste

Yields **2** generous servings

1. Fill a saucepan with water and bring to boil over high heat. Add sausages and reduce heat to low. Cover and simmer until cooked through, about 4-8 minutes depending on size. Remove and drain. Allow to cool and cut into ½" lengths. In a heavy skillet over medium-high heat, add a tsp of cooking oil and sauté the sausages pieces, tossing them so they brown on all sides. When nicely browned, remove from heat and set aside.

2. In a mixing bowl, beat together eggs and cream with salt and pepper to taste, according to the saltiness of the sausages.

3. Melt 1 Tbsp butter in the sauté pan over medium heat and pour in the eggs. Reduce heat to medium-low. Shake pan gently back and forth to allow cooked eggs to gather up in clumps. Sprinkle in cooked sausage and, using a large fork, gently lift the cooked eggs up so the raw eggs can run under to the bottom of the pan. Work in light, fluffing movements over medium-low heat. When eggs are almost all cooked – you should still see the glossiness of some uncooked egg – fluff them one more time and turn them out onto two plates. The eggs will continue to cook in their own heat so the rawness will disappear but they will still be moist. Serve with lightly toasted baguettes and peach-almond jam or nestled in halved croissants and garnished with fruit.

HIGH LIFE EGGS (104)

Hannibal takes his recipe for High Life Eggs from *El Practicón*, the classic Spanish treatise on food written by Angel Muro in the19th century. The recipe is historically enduring, it seems. High Life Eggs quickly became one of the most-requested recipes in all the seasons of *Hannibal*. Not surprising – it's addictively rich and crunchy on the bottom and creamy-eggy on the top. Plus it's super easy to make!

INGREDIENTS:

2 slices heavy Italian or Portuguese
 white bread, 1" thick
2 eggs
salt and pepper to taste
olive oil for frying

Yields **2** servings

1. Using a small glass or round cookie cutter, with the slices flat on your table surface, cut a circle out of each slice of bread but not all the way through. Form a shallow cup in each slice by pulling bread out of cut circle leaving about ¼" layer of bread intact on the bottom.

2. Crack each egg into a small bowl or cup and set aside.

3. In heavy skillet large enough to hold both slices of bread, heat olive oil for shallow-frying (about 1" deep). When oil starts to shimmer, toss in a cube of bread. If it browns in 30 seconds, the oil is the right temperature. Remove test bread cube and put the slices of bread, hole side up in the oil. Immediately pour one egg into each hole and cook until egg white is set. The edges of the bread will get a bit burnt but this is part of the flavour. Gently remove from oil with a slotted spatula and drain on paper towels. Place on individual plates and season with salt and pepper. Serve with tomato salsa if desired.

BREAKFAST WITH DADDY

In *Oeuf* (season 1, episode 4), Hannibal comforts traumatized Abigail. He plays to her subconscious by making breakfast for her exactly as her father had when he was brutally shot in front of her. Eggs, fruit, sausages, and, oh…that's just psilocybin tea.

   The script called for "High Life Eggs" and I made them from elegant braided buns because they reflected the twisted beauty of Hannibal. Sort of. Truth be told, I used those buns because we had four big food scenes to shoot that day and I had forgotten to bring bread. Challah buns were all we could find in the supermarket close to the studio, but they worked beautifully, their twisted tops adding dimension to what otherwise would have looked like a kid's Egg in a Hole. Much better than plain sliced bread. Sometimes you get lucky…

HANGTOWN FRY (205)

Preparing breakfast, coffee and comfort for Jack Crawford, Hannibal assembles the rich ingredients: suspiciously large oysters, home-smoked bacon and farm-fresh eggs.

INGREDIENTS:

4 eggs
3 Tbsp cream

¼ cup water
6 raw oysters, shucked
¾ cup Panko breadcrumbs
¼ cup flour
6 Tbsp butter

4 thick slices pancetta bacon, fried
salt, pepper

Yields **2** servings

1. In a mixing bowl, beat eggs and cream together. Remove 2 Tbsp to a second bowl. Set first bowl aside while you fry the oysters.

2. In the second bowl, add ¼ cup water to the 2 Tbsp egg mixture and beat together.

3. Spread breadcrumbs on a plate and flour on another plate.

4. Coat each oyster with flour, then dip in egg water, then roll in breadcrumbs to coat evenly.

5. In a skillet over medium-high heat, melt 2 Tbsp of butter and sauté oysters on both sides just until golden brown. Do not cook all the way through. Set aside.

6. Wipe skillet clean with paper towel and place over medium heat. Add remaining butter. When butter is bubbling, add eggs from first bowl. Season with salt and pepper to taste. Scramble by stirring eggs gently with a fork and when egg is partially cooked, add oysters. Continue to scramble gently and just as eggs are becoming fully cooked but still glossy with a bit of liquid egg, turn out onto two plates. Garnish with bacon slices and serve.

JUGGLING EGGS FOR JACK

The script for *Mukozuke* (season 2, episode 5) described Hannibal executing a knife trick with an egg that had my whole department in a sweat. I had seen Benihana chefs botch this trick and I knew how difficult it was. We wanted to get it right and, on the day of the shoot, had two Japanese chefs, a wide selection of knives and spatulas, and a gross of eggs on set. Our two chefs spent the morning in make-up and wardrobe getting their hands ready to stand in for Mads. I paced beside my prep tables counting eggs and lines of dialogue to reassure myself that 12 dozen eggs would cover the number of "takes" required.

When it was finally time to shoot the scene, Mads strolled over and casually asked what he was supposed to do. I carefully explained the action and added that although the trick was extremely difficult, he needn't be worried because we had back-up hand-doubles who could step in if he had any trouble.

He picked up a spatula, tossed an egg in the air and cracked it perfectly as it descended on the edge of the spatula - contents slurping into the bowl below. "Like that?" he asked with a sly grin. As I shook my head disbelievingly, he explained he had done a lot of juggling in his youth, so this egg thing was a breeze. They got the shot in one take.

USING YOUR BRAINS IN THE KITCHEN

The kitchen scenes were always a delight to shoot – Mads had a way of handling the food and equipment that made him look like an accomplished chef. Even when the script called for something questionable (Putting raw kidneys through the meat grinder? Really?) Mikkelsen pulled it off with aplomb. I don't think he ever got a wayward spot on his apron or nicked his finger in the three years of kitchen scenes using even the most wicked-looking implements.

We had footage of Mads lovingly cooking thymus and liver for another episode but the corresponding dinner scenes were cut. The unused shots were beautiful, like tasty leftovers left to cool in the back of the fridge, so, wanting to make use of them in another episode, Bryan Fuller asked for a dish Hannibal might make with those ingredients.

Robyn Stern – José André's resourceful research assistant – came up with a recipe for La Tortilla Sacromonte. José, always dreaming of magical scenarios, added that Hannibal could say that he lived with Andalusian gypsies for a time and they taught him many valuable life lessons including how to make this Spanish omelette using brain, sweetbreads, testicles and liver.

TORTILLA SACROMONTE (209)

A Spanish tortilla is made the same way as Italian frittata: ingredients are sliced and layered with egg in a deep-dish omelette. The important thing is to not overcook it or the moisture will be driven out of the eggs and they will become spongy in texture. Lamb testicles can taste quite muttony so use beef, chicken or pork testicles if you want a more delicate flavour.

INGREDIENTS:

1 lamb brain
1 bay leaf
½ tsp dried Fines Herbes*
1 lamb testicle
salt and pepper to taste
1 Tbsp olive oil

1 large cooked potato, cut in ⅛" thick
   slices
¼ cup chopped red bell pepper

6 eggs, beaten
¼ cup cream or milk

*Fines Herbes is a blend of fragrant
herbs that you can buy pre-mixed or
make yourself by combining equal parts
parsley, chives, chervil and tarragon.

Yields **6** servings

1. Prepare brains: Peel apart the two brain halves and set aside. In a medium saucepan with cold water, add Fines Herbes, bay leaf and bring to boil. Reduce heat to simmer and add brain. Poach gently for 8-10 minutes. Remove with slotted spoon and plunge into cold water until cooled all the way through. Drain well. Pull apart into segments about 2" in diameter, discarding connective membrane. Sprinkle with salt and pepper and set aside.

2. Prepare testicle: Cut a slash in the outer membrane and gently peel membrane off the soft inside meat. Remove outer membrane completely and discard, keeping the soft inside in a whole piece. Cut through inner membrane and peel by running your finger under the surface of the membrane to separate it from the meat. Discard this inner membrane. Cover skinned testicle in salted water (½ tsp salt per cup of water) and brine for 6 hours or overnight, changing to fresh salt-water after the first 3 hours. Drain and poach in simmering water for 10-12 minutes just to firm up the meat a bit. Do not overcook or the meat will shrink and become overly intense in flavour. Remove, cool and slice into ½" thick rounds. Sprinkle with salt and pepper and set aside.

3. Assemble omelette: Beat eggs in a large bowl with milk. Add salt and pepper to taste. Heat the remaining oil in large, non-stick omelette pan over a medium-low heat. Pour in ⅓ of the beaten eggs and layer in the half of the potatoes. Add half the brains, testicles and peppers in an even layer. Pour over another third of the egg and layer in the rest of the brain, testicle and peppers pressing ingredients down into the pan to flatten the top. Layer on the rest of the potato slices and pour in the remaining egg and continue cooking over medium-low heat till mostly set then place it under the broiler only until the top is freckled with brown.

SALSA in
WILD DUCK
EGGSHELL

grilled
baby orange

purple
potatos

liver + sweetbread
frittata

wasabi mustard cream

CHICKEN CHEESE FRITTATA

Prepping for the Sacromonte eating scene, I didn't think Laurence and Mads would want to spend the morning eating fried brains and testicles so I substituted chicken when I made the omelettes for the shoot. Olé! They ate it up with gusto!

Here's the recipe so if the FBI ever drops in unexpectedly, absence of balls and brains notwithstanding, you can satisfy inquiring agents with a wedge of this:

INGREDIENTS:

6 eggs
¼ cup cream
¼ tsp salt, pepper to taste

1 Tbsp butter
1 large cooked potato, in ⅛" slices
½ medium onion, in ¼" slices, pan-fried
   until translucent
½ cup cooked chicken in ½" dice
½ cup peas
½ cup diced red bell peppers
2 oz Gruyere cheese thinly sliced
¼ cup grated Parmesan cheese

Yields **6** servings

1. In a mixing bowl, beat eggs with cream, salt and pepper.

2. Over medium heat, melt butter in a 10" omelette pan or other non-stick slope-sided frying pan. When butter is bubbling and beginning to brown, pour in a third of the beaten egg to cover bottom of pan. In a single layer, add half of the potato slices and sprinkle in half of the chicken, half of the onions and half of the cheese. Pour over another third of egg then layer in the remaining fillings. Pour the remaining egg over all to the top of the omelette pan and sprinkle Parmesan over top.

3. Continue cooking over medium-low heat until egg has mostly set then place under broiler to finish cooking egg and brown the top slightly.

4. Cut into wedges and serve with a salad. If you have any left over, this is also great eaten cold right out of the fridge. Remember: anything eaten standing in front of the fridge has no calories.

BROKEN TEACUP PARFAIT

A bigail drops the teacup, shattering it. Sadly, until Hannibal figures out how to reverse entropy, the teacup remains broken. So make the best of it – turn that visual trope into a no-bake fruit crumble that can be served with yogurt for breakfast or with ice cream as dessert. For an even easier preparation, substitute granola for the no-bake crumble.

INGREDIENTS:

4 small round balloons
8 oz white chocolate compound wafers

½ cup instant oatmeal
2 Tbsp butter
1 Tbsp sugar

1 cup lemon flavoured yoghurt
1 cup mixed berries such as raspberries,
    blueberries, blackberries
honey to drizzle

Yields 4 servings

TO MAKE TEACUPS:

1. Line a cookie sheet or baking tray with parchment and set aside. Place white chocolate wafers in a bowl over a pot of gently simmering water and stir occasionally until melted and smooth.

2. Wash and dry balloons, then inflate until they are about 2" diameter. Knot the top and dip the other end of each balloon into the chocolate, swirling to coat each balloon half-way up. Using the back of a spoon or a small spatula, remove excess chocolate so each balloon bottom is covered in an even thin film of chocolate. If chocolate is too stiff, thin out with ½ tsp vegetable oil or warm it more. Stand the balloons up, chocolate end down on cookie pan. The chocolate should pool a little at the bottom so balloons will stand up straight. Put in fridge to harden.

3. When chocolate is cool and completely firm, snip a small hole in each balloon to slowly deflate, then gently peel balloons out of chocolate.

TO MAKE CRUMBLE:

1. In a sauté pan over medium-high heat, melt butter. Add oatmeal and stir to blend. Sprinkle in sugar and stir quickly with a spatula until sugar melts and oatmeal browns. Remove from heat, spread oatmeal on a plate and set aside to cool.

TO ASSEMBLE:

1. Place each cup on individual plates and fill each chocolate cup with ¼ cup of yoghurt and top with ¼ cup of berries. Pressing sides with fingers, break each cup into 3 or 4 fragments. Sprinkle each with Crumble, drizzle with honey and serve.

HAVING FRIENDS
FOR DINNER

APPETIZERS

Broken heart or squab toes, anyone? Anyone? Even when you're gripped with fear, Hannibal has a way of whetting your appetite. Whether he's giving a grand dinner in *Sorbet* (season 1, episode 7), a cocktail party in *Futamono* (season 2, episode 6) or simply seducing someone special, he's got a recipe for everyone and everyone in a recipe.

HEART TARTARE TARTS (206)

Haven't got the heart? You can substitute chopped beef tenderloin in this recipe, or if you prefer pescatarian you can substitute chopped raw salmon or tuna (sushi grade, of course). Instead of filo shard shells, you can make easy barquette style tart shells from frozen puff pastry (p79).

INGREDIENTS:

For heart tartare:
½ lb veal heart, very finely chopped
1 tsp olive oil
1 tsp capers
1 tsp chopped cornichon pickles
1 tsp red onions, finely chopped
salt, pepper to taste

For tart shells:
6 sheets filo dough (approx 12" x 18")
½ cup melted butter

Yields **12** tarts

TO MAKE TARTARE:

1. Remove all silverskin, veins and connective tendons (the Chordae Tendineae - also called Heart Strings, and yes, they do break).

2. Combine chopped heart, oil, cornichons, onions, capers, salt and pepper. Refrigerate until just before serving.

TO MAKE PASTRY SHELLS:

1. Brush 1 sheet of filo dough with butter and place two more sheets directly on top. Brush the top with butter and layer on two more sheets. Butter the top layer and add remaining sheet. Press lightly to stick layers together. Cut the stacked filo into 12 squares 3" x 3", reserving offcuts for shards. Press squares into a buttered mini muffin tin creating a cup in each one for the filling and allowing corners of pastry to extend up from sides of each cup. Bake at 375°F until lightly browned, about 5 minutes.

2. Set aside to cool. Fill each shell with 1-2 tsp heart tartare just before serving.

TO MAKE DECORATIVE SHARDS:

1. Cut pastry scraps into long triangular shards and place on buttered cookie sheet. Bake at 375°F until golden brown. Set aside to cool. Spear into filled tart shells just before serving.

LAMB FRIES (105)

Because…someone is careless and loses his testicles in Scene 16 of *Coquilles* (season 1, episode 5). You may only have one pair of testicles but you can't have too many testicle recipes.

Tenderly creamy in texture and tasting like lamb-flavoured sweetbreads, these are deep-fried and actually pretty tasty. (Well, no big surprise – anything deep-fried is delicious. Especially with a side of French-fried potatoes – might as well do some while the oil is hot.) Confession: the quantities given are approximate but you can use this recipe as a guideline. As is often the case in life, the size of your testicles will determine in part how it all pans out.

INGREDIENTS:

1 pair lamb's testicles

2 Tbsp flour for dredging
1 egg yolk with water added to yield
⅛ cup
1 tsp sesame seeds, optional
½ tsp Fines Herbes
¼ cup Panko Japanese breadcrumbs or
other breadcrumb
¼ tsp salt

1 lemon, cut in wedges
baby salad greens
oil for deep-frying

1. Peel testicles: Using the tip of a very sharp pair of scissors, snip open the outer membrane and slit open the membrane top to bottom and slip out the testicle. There are two more layers of membrane but you can peel them off as one. Using scissor tips, slit the membrane open from top to bottom, taking care not to cut into the meat. Separate the membrane by sliding the edge of a teaspoon between the meat and the membrane, scraping along the membrane to avoid damaging the egg-shaped flesh inside. Excess blood vessels, tube and lobe will come away with the membrane as you pull it off.

2. Transfer meat to bowl and cover with lightly salted water (½ tsp salt to 1 cup water) and soak refrigerated for 8 hr or overnight. Change to fresh salt water every few hours until the water stays clear. Place meat in saucepan over medium-high heat and cover with cold water. Allow water to begin to boil, then reduce heat to low. Simmer for 15 minutes. Remove, drain and cover with cold water. Meat can be held in the refrigerator at this stage for 1-2 days.

3. To fry, cut meat lengthwise into ½"x½"x2" strips about the size of French fries and set aside. In a small bowl, beat yolk and water together and set aside. In a small bowl, combine flour, herbs and sesame seeds. Five or six at a time, drop the "fries" into the flour and toss to coat evenly. Remove and repeat with remaining pieces. Add breadcrumbs to the flour mixture and stir to mix well. A few at a time, dip the floured fries into the egg mixture to coat completely, then drop into first bowl and toss to coat well in breadcrumbs. Remove and repeat until all fries are coated.

4. Heat oil to 375° or until a cube of white bread dropped in the oil turns golden-brown in 6 seconds. Drop a small handful of breadcrumbed meat into the hot oil and deep-fry until golden brown. Remove from oil with slotted spoon or spider and drain on paper towel. Repeat with remaining meat. Between batches, keep oil clear by skimming out any loose bits with a spider or small strainer. Arrange lamb fries on a bed of baby salad greens, sprinkle with salt and lemon juice. Serve with lemon wedges. Bone appétit!

SEARED FOIE GRAS WITH SAGE PLUM BERRY SAUCE (105)

I n one of our first glimpses of our cannibal's fondness for puns, Dr Lecter purrs to Jack, "I'd love to have you both for dinner." Fast-forward a few episodes and Jack with his wife, Bella, are sitting at the good doctor's table discussing humane animal husbandry. Foie gras is cruel, she asserts, declining to partake of the appetizer. Oh Bella, if you only knew the half of it…

This is a quick version of the appetizer Hannibal serves Jack and Bella. Cooking foie gras by searing is a much easier preparation than making a classic torchon. Hannibal serves a Fig Vidal sauce with dry and fresh figs; I have chosen to serve with a Sage Plum Berry Sauce, the recipe for which is on page 32.

INGREDIENTS:

½ lobe duck foie gras (about ½ lb)
¼ cup flour
sea salt, freshly ground black pepper
   to taste
½ tsp butter
balsamic vinegar glaze* (optional)

*Balsamic vinegar glaze or glacé is balsamic vinegar that has been reduced to a thick, sweet syrup. You can buy it by the bottle or you can make your own by gently boiling balsamic vinegar until it reduces in volume and has acquired the consistency of corn syrup.

Serves **4** generous appetizer portions

1. Remove foie from refrigerator and let stand 20 minutes or just until pliable. Using the tip of a knife, carefully remove veins and discard, keeping liver intact. Cut in slices about ½" thick. Dredge in flour and sprinkle lightly with salt and pepper. Refrigerate or freeze until ready to sear and serve.

2. Ten minutes before serving, heat sauté pan over high heat. Add butter and, just as butter browns, add 5 or 6 slices of foie to the pan – do not crowd them. Sear quickly, just until browned on both sides. The slices will release some fat but do not cook too long or all the delicious fat will melt out. The slices should still be rare in the middle. Repeat with remaining slices.

3. Drizzle slices with balsamic glaze. Serve immediately with Sage Plum Berry Sauce (p32) and toasted brioche.

• cockfeathers garnish w mini purple cabbage

• Foie Torchon slices
• Radiccio
• Fig Balsamic Drizzle

SAGE PLUM BERRY SAUCE

T his is a fruity sauce that goes well with foie gras, but it is also excellent with poultry, pork or ham.
You can also drizzle it on toast slathered with triple crème cheese or you can feed it to vegetarian
vampires, as I did for a scene in *Hemlock Grove*.

Produced by Gaumont at the same time as *Hannibal*, *Hemlock Grove* was shooting just down the street.
It was a series about a young vampire prince who would be seized by sudden urgings to consume raw
bloody meat. So they called on me whenever their scripts called for blood-spurting hearts or kidneys or
raw sausages that drooled with blood when the actor bit into them. I would create hearts made out of jelly
and hollow sausages made of beets and breadcrumbs and fill them with thinned Plum Berry Sauce for the
goriest, goopiest, gobby-est, tastiest blood-spurt ever. Horrifyingly delicious!

INGREDIENTS:

one 10-oz can cranberry (whole berry)
   sauce
2 Tbsp red wine vinegar
3 prune plums pitted and cut in ¼"
   cubes
2 red plums pitted and cut in ¼" cubes
3-4 sprigs fresh sage

Yields **2** cups

1. In a small saucepan over medium-high heat, combine cranberry sauce, vinegar,
plum chunks and sage. Reduce heat to low and simmer until plums are softened
but not mushy. Remove sage sprigs. Can be stored in refrigerator for a week or
frozen for several months.

FOIE GRAS AU TORCHON (105)

The first foie gras scene, in which Hannibal has Jack and his wife for dinner, was a delight to shoot. Mads thoroughly enjoyed the foie and Gina Torres was happy with her fake foie – she didn't want to eat the real thing because of the cruelty involved in force-feeding ducks to engorge their livers.

I made foie gras again for Hugh's scene with Hannibal and the ortolans. Referencing the dying President Mitterrand's infamous last meal of foie gras and ortolans, I prepared a starter of Foie Gras au Torchon. Hugh ate 3 or 4 plattersful in the process of filming the moment and pronounced it quite delicious.

This takes time and effort to prepare foie this way but the smooth texture is really wonderful. Don't overcook it or you will be left with a sad tiny piece of liver and a big pool of expensive duck fat.

INGREDIENTS:

1 lobe fresh duck foie gras (about 1 lb)
1 cup Madeira, port or brandy

Yields about **12** slices

1. Marinate liver in Madeira in a zip-lock plastic bag overnight. Remove liver and pat dry. Allow to soften at room temperature for about 20 minutes. Remove veins with the tip of sharp knife. Keep the liver intact. Sprinkle with sea salt. Using a clean linen towel lined with plastic wrap, (that's the "torchon" part – French for towel) roll the liver, and squeeze it into a cylinder shape about 2" diameter. Pull away the towel and plastic wrap and re-wrap the liver in more plastic wrap, rolling it tightly in 4 or 5 layers. Twist the ends closed and tie tightly with kitchen string. Wrap again with a few more layers of plastic wrap to seal the liver in a watertight casing.

2. Over high heat, bring water to boil in a pot large enough to contain the liver roll. Reduce heat to maintain a water temperature of 130°F. Put liver roll in water and poach for 25-30 minutes. Remove and refrigerate at least 4 hours until firm. Peel off plastic wrap and cut liver in ½" slices. Sprinkle with sea salt and drizzle with balsamic glacé. Serve cold with Sage Plum Berry Sauce (p32) and brioche toast.

CHICKEN LIVER PÂTÉ TORCHON

Here is a smooth delicious pâté that is an inexpensive but worthy stand-in for the costly Foie Gras Torchon that Hannibal burns through as if it's rude chopped liver – oh, wait…

INGREDIENTS:

1 small onion, chopped

1 lb chicken livers
½ lb pork liver, cut into ½" strips
¼ tsp dried rubbed sage
6 Tbsp cognac, madeira or sherry
¾ cup butter, softened
½ cup firm cream cheese, softened
salt and pepper to taste

2 empty washed 12-oz frozen juice
    cardboard cans
or paper coffee cups prepared as
    described in Faux Foie Torchon (p76)

Yields **6-8** appetizers

1. In a sauté pan heat a heaped soupspoon of the butter over medium-low heat. Add onions and sauté until translucent and golden (10-15 minutes). Transfer to bowl and set aside.

2. Increase heat to medium-high and add a heaped soupspoon of the butter and the pork liver slivers to sauté pan, tossing to brown on all sides just until cooked, about 3 minutes. Do not overcook. Liver should still be pinkish inside. Transfer to bowl of cooked onions to cool. Deglaze pan by adding 2 Tbsp of cognac and bringing to gentle boil and scraping up all the bits from bottom of pan as cognac bubbles. Using a rubber spatula, transfer all pan juices and bits into bowl of cooked liver, scraping the pan clean. Return pan to heat. Add another spoonful of the butter and half of the chicken livers to the pan and sauté until just cooked, about 3 minutes. Transfer to bowl of cooked livers, deglaze pan and repeat with remaining chicken livers. Add salt, pepper and sage to taste and toss together. Set aside to cool.

3. In a food processor, chop livers and onions until coarsely chopped. Add remaining butter and cream cheese and purée until smooth and well-blended. Press into empty washed 10-oz frozen juice containers and refrigerate for at least 2 hours until pâté is firm. Peel away sides of container and cut pâté into ½" slices. Serve with Sage Plum Berry Sauce (p32) and toast triangles or bagel chips.

Foie Gras Timbits (206)

Opening his home for an elegant cocktail party, Hannibal served these little bites to guests both suspicious and unsuspecting. Gossiping about the liver, many were starting to clue in on Hannibal's penchant for people meat – but they had no idea he was serving them donut Timbits from the local Tim Horton's Coffee shop. The horror!

INGREDIENTS:

12 donut "holes" or vanilla cake pops
4 oz pâté de foie gras or Chicken Liver
   Pâté Torchon
4 Tbsp red current jelly

Yields **24** hors d'oeuvres

1. Slice donut holes in half. Cut foie gras pâté into slices ½" thick and then into ½" triangles. Place donut hole halves on platter cut side up and a triangle of foie gras on each. Top with a dab of jelly and serve.

THE
MANY OYSTERS
OF SEASON 3

While living with Hannibal in Florence, Bedelia eats raw oysters as a way of ensuring that she is not dining on murder victims. In flashbacks, Gideon is forced to eat oysters to improve the flavour of his flesh as Hannibal cooks him limb by severed limb. Turning the tables, Verger feeds oysters to Hannibal to enhance his flavour, but also because he secretly longs to be just like Hannibal. We went through beds of bivalves shooting these scenes. Season 3 was not a good year to be an oyster!

It was fun doing these scenes because it was like having an oyster bar in the sound stage. Prodigious amounts of molluscs were shucked and slurped in the name of cinema. Matt Woo, our oyster guru, helped us by supplying just the right oysters for each scene. For Gillian Andersen, he brought Marina's Top Drawers, the plump and creamy Pacific variety named after Cortes' gun-toting mistress. She adored them and astounded us by sliding back several dozen when we shot her scenes.

TIPS FOR BUYING AND STORING OYSTERS

Buying: Your grandpa's rule of "no oysters in months without an r" doesn't really stand any longer. Oysters are flown in from all around the world so they are always being freshly harvested somewhere. Get your oysters from a reliable fishmonger that specializes in shellfish. Choose oysters whose shells are tightly closed and not chipped or cracked. They should smell as clean and fresh as ocean air.

Storing: Just-harvested oysters will stay fresh for a week if properly stored. Wash them under running water with a vegetable brush, removing all sand and debris, then place them flat side facing up, wrap in wet newspaper with some wet seaweed and store in the fridge in a cardboard box. Do not submerge them in water or store them on ice as this will kill them.

Varieties: Atlantic oysters are salty and crisp; Pacific tend to be larger, creamy and sweet. Their size and texture depends on the temperature of their beds and, although their species has some influence, because of the gallons of water they filter as they feed, their flavour depends almost entirely on the water of their locale. As Hannibal is always espousing, you taste like what you eat and oysters are a prime example of this. Brackish waters will result in a salty crisp metallic flavours and fresh water will result in a sweet rounded taste.

FRESH OYSTERS WITH MIGNONETTE SAUCE (302)

M ads always liked to have hot sauce with his oysters. For Gillian, we made Mignonette Sauce because qu'elle est mignonne! I made a little dish out of oyster shells for the sauce (p224) that you can easily replicate for your sauce dish or use for candle holders.

INGREDIENTS:

¼ cup white wine vinegar
¼ cup white Balsamic vinegar
6 Tbsp chopped shallots
2 tsp coarsely ground peppercorns
⅛ tsp salt

Yields ¾ cup sauce

1. In a small bowl combine all ingredients and refrigerate for at least 2 hours. Serve in a bowl with a small spoon as a garnish for freshly shucked oysters on the half-shell. This is also great on sliced tomatoes.

OYSTERS VERGERFELLER (307)

With Hannibal strapped into a wheelchair at the Verger dinner table, Mason delights in the idea of fattening him on oysters. His chef Cordell is thrilled to show off his somewhat bourgeois culinary skills so he makes a sumptuous version of the already super-rich Oysters Rockefeller. He serves them with a red pepper salsa although they require nothing more than a squirt of lemon or a drop of hot sauce. Hannibal eschews the cooked oysters and just nibbles on the salsa, his elitism unfettered by his compromised position.

INGREDIENTS:

12 oysters freshly shucked, top (flat) shell discarded

1 cup (packed) baby spinach, washed (about 3 oz)
1 green onion finely chopped
2 Tbsp mayonnaise
½ tsp Italian Herb mix*
salt, pepper to taste

2 Tbsp Panko style breadcrumbs
1 Tbsp grated Parmesan cheese
⅛ tsp smoked paprika (optional)

Lemon to garnish

*Italian Herb mix is a blend of oregano, basil, rosemary, thyme and sometimes sage or marjoram and garlic powder. You can substitute Italian branch oregano.

Yields **2** appetizers

1. Prepare spinach mix: In a plastic zippered bag, microwave spinach for 40 seconds, or until wilted. Cool, squeeze out liquid and chop finely. It should yield about ⅓ cup. Transfer to a bowl and add green onion, mayonnaise, herbs and salt, mixing until well blended.

2. Prepare breadcrumb mix: In a second bowl, mix together breadcrumbs, cheese and paprika.

3. Line a broiling pan with lightly crumpled aluminum foil. Place shucked oysters on pan, pressing into foil so the shells do not tip in the tray. Spread a spoonful of spinach mix over each oyster and sprinkle breading mix on top to cover spinach. Broil just until breadcrumbs have browned and oysters have warmed through with edges curling, 8-10 minutes. The oysters should be barely cooked. Transfer to serving platter and garnish with slices of lemon.

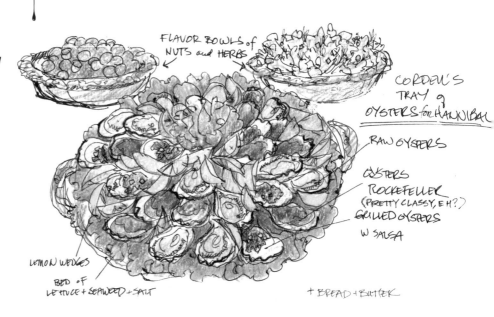

FLAVOR BOWLS of NUTS and HERBS

CORDELL'S TRAY of OYSTERS for HANNIBAL

RAW OYSTERS

OYSTERS ROCKEFELLER (PRETTY CLASSY, EH?)

GRILLED OYSTERS W SALSA

LEMON WEDGES

BED of LETTUCE + SEAWEED + SALT

+ BREAD + BUTTER

GRILLED OCTOPUS

Robyn Stern, José Andrés clever research assistant, gave me her secret Spanish recipe for cooking octopus: Bring to boil a big pot of water, salted like the sea, and throw the octopus in. Count to three and pull it out. Let the water come to boil again and back in with the octopus. Count three. Out. Repeat three times. Then you grill it or roast it over an open fire. I think you are supposed to be barefoot by a sunny sea with your Spanish cousins as you do this.

My able assistant, John Kruusi, did it a different way for Hannibal's table. Even though there was much less counting, and it was grilled in the dark of Ontario's winter in a cold studio, his octopus was redolent of Robyn's sunny Spain.

INGREDIENTS:

1 medium-sized frozen octopus (7-8 lb), thawed
1 large onion, quartered
1 bay leaf
½ cup olive oil
2 Tbsp smoked paprika
¼ cup caper berries, drained
¼ cup flat-leaf parsley, rough chopped
2 limes, cut in wedges
salt, pepper to taste

Yields appetizer for **6**

1. Bring a large pot of lightly salted water to boil over medium-high heat. Add the octopus and return to boil, allowing it to cook for 2 additional minutes. Remove and when cool enough to handle, cut off head, beak and any loose skin, torn suckers, remaining innards and discard. You should be left with lovely fat coiling tentacles and the collar.

2. Heat the pot of water over medium again and when it begins to boil, add the octopus meat and reduce the heat to low. Simmer gently for 1½ hours, turning tentacles occasionally to ensure even cooking. Remove, cool and cut into bite-sized pieces.

3. 3 In a large heavy skillet, add olive oil over medium-high heat. Add octopus pieces and sauté quickly on each side to brown. Remove from pan and arrange on serving platter. Sprinkle with paprika and scatter parsley and caper berries over all. Season with salt and pepper, garnish with lime wedges and serve.

ESCARGOT BOURGUIGNONNE (301)

Season 3 opens with snails and fireflies doing their worst to consume everything in their path - but in the end, being consumed themselves. We had no end of snail diversion during the long hours on set – organizing snail races…supervising snail naps… having informative chats with the snail wrangler. (Yes, that's a job. A wrangler is a specialist hired to handle animals on a film set. We had many – including a maggot wrangler for Oeuf in season 1, episode 4.)

Poor Gideon has his arm eaten by snails as it hangs, dripping with marinade in a glass-encased cochlear garden tucked in Hannibal's subterranean wine cave. The arm-flavoured snails are then served to Gideon who is just crazy enough to try them. This was one of my favourite culinary concoctions. I was delighted that such a gruesome concept could spring from my mind - so preoccupied as it is with the prettier parts of life. And even more delighted when the scriptwriters ran with the concept. (S)nailed it!

Escargots have been enjoyed by kings and paupers since pre-history. Ancient Romans considered snails an elite food and, as early as 42 BC created cochlear gardens where they bred and fed their snails on herbs, cornmeal and wine. They raised varieties of snails on vegetation specifically cultivated to enhance each species' flavour. Their popularity waxes and wanes but snails endure as a much-loved delicacy.

In France during the mid-1900s, MFK Fisher wrote of grape harvesters stopping in the hot afternoon for a break, setting a small fire in a patch of grass, then picking through the burnt foliage, pulling out the charred shells and feasting on hot juicy nuggets of grape-fattened field-roasted snails washed down with juice squeezed from over-ripe grapes.

In lieu of Burgundian fields overrun with drunken gastropods, try this simple but delicious preparation using canned snails.

INGREDIENTS:

one 8-oz can of prepared Burgundian
   snails, drained
24 clean snail shells
¾ cup butter
¼ cup flat-leaf parsley, chopped
3 cloves garlic, minced
salt to taste

2 baguettes

Yields appetizer for **2-3**

1. In a small bowl, beat butter until soft and light. Add parsley, garlic and salt.

2. Place a dollop of butter in each shell and push one snail into each shell. Press more butter into each shell. Place one stuffed shell in each divot on 4 snail plates.

3. Bake at 350°F for 10 minutes. Serve with sliced baguettes for mopping up the sauce.

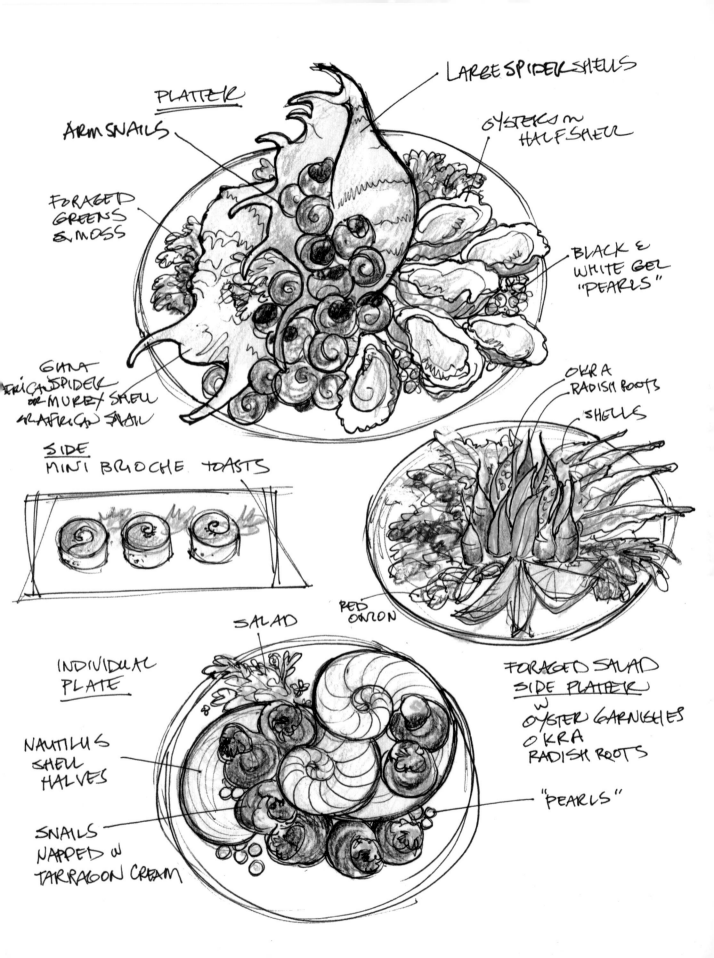

PLATTER

LARGE SPIDER SHELLS

ARM SNAILS

OYSTERS on HALF SHELL

FORAGED GREENS & MOSS

BLACK & WHITE GEL "PEARLS"

GIANT AFRICAN SPIDER or MUREX SHELL w/AFRICAN SNAIL

SIDE
MINI BRIOCHE TOASTS

OKRA
RADISH ROOTS

SHELLS

RED ONION

SALAD

INDIVIDUAL PLATE

FORAGED SALAD
SIDE PLATTER
w
OYSTER GARNISHES
OKRA
RADISH ROOTS

NAUTILUS
SHELL
HALVES

"PEARLS"

SNAILS
NAPPED w
TARRAGON CREAM

BEDELIA'S BELLYBUTTONS WITH ABSINTHE CREAM (304)

S hirtless, Hannibal feeds snails to Bedelia – some are on skewers and some are nestled in mushroom caps like brown buttered belly buttons. For the scene, I had set the prepared escargots on a large platter with a little plate and fork each for the two of them. But Mads had a better idea.

Perhaps inspired by those sexy scenes in old Hollywood movies where the manly-man puts two cigarettes in his lips, lights both and passes one to his paramour, Mads thought that I should put two snails on a skewer and he would pull one off with his teeth, then feed the other to Bedelia. Perfect. Later, live-tweeting with the broadcast, Bryan would post my concept sketch dubbing the dish "Post-coital Snails" and momentarily breaking Twitter.

INGREDIENTS:

Bellybuttons:
one 8-oz can Burgundian snails, drained
24 white mushrooms about 1½" diameter
3 Tbsp butter
1 clove garlic, chopped
salt, to taste

Yields **2-3** appetizer-sized servings

Absinthe Cream:
1 cup whipping cream
3–4 sprigs fresh tarragon, chopped, stems removed
1 Tbsp Absinthe or Pernod (optional)
salt, to taste

Yields ⅔ cup sauce

BELLYBUTTONS:

1. Wash mushrooms gently, pat dry with paper towels, then remove the stems. Reserve the stems for use at another time – perhaps to add to a sauce, soup or stew.

2. Melt butter in skillet over medium heat. Add garlic and mushroom caps and cook for 2 minutes on each side just until mushrooms start to brown. Add snails and toss just until snails are hot and mushrooms begin to release their juices. Salt to taste and remove from heat.

3. Remove mushrooms and snails from skillet, placing 6 mushroom caps upside down on each plate, place one snail in the stem cup of each mushroom cap. Spoon any pan juices over the snails. Serve with Absinthe cream and crusty bread.

ABSINTHE CREAM:

1. Heat small sauté pan over high heat and add cream, tarragon and absinthe. Boil, stirring constantly until reduced by a third and thickened, about 8 to 10 minutes. Set aside, keeping warm until ready to serve. If sauce thickens too much, whisk in a bit of whipping cream or white wine to correct the consistency. Add salt if desired. Spoon over warm snails.

CAJUN FRIED FROGS' LEGS WITH PISTACHIO DUST (304)

In an alternate reality of Will, Jack and Hannibal's stabbing dinner, Hannibal presents hors d'oeuvres to Will. The script called for two plates from which Will could choose. For one, I suggested frogs' legs to represent Aesop's fabled scorpion who stung the frog to death after he had ferried him to safety, because, like Hannibal, "that's what scorpions do".

As we shot it, the scene was changed and my lovely platter of frogs' legs wasn't required so I offered it to Hugh Dancy as he stopped by my tables between takes. When he went back to set licking his lips, Laurence and Mads wanted some too, so I gave them a platter and we had a little break while they devoured them all with glee. Much joking of French cuisine ensued: Laurence, Mads and Hugh always brought their wonderful humour to the sound stage which was why we all loved working with them.

INGREDIENTS:

8 pair medium-sized frogs' legs, skins removed

For marinade:
1 egg, beaten
½ cup milk
1 Tbsp Creole spice mix (below)

For breading:
¼ cup flour
¾ cup Panko breadcrumbs
1 Tbsp spice mix

To garnish:
2 Tbsp pistachio nuts, chopped
4 lemon wedges

Yields **4** appetizer-sized servings

1. In a plastic zipper storage bag, combine egg, milk and 1 Tbsp of the spice mix. Add frogs' legs, zip closed and marinate refrigerated for 1 hour.

2. In another plastic bag, combine flour, breadcrumbs and 1 Tbsp spice mix. Remove 1 pair frog's legs from marinade and shake of excess liquid. Drop into bag with breadcrumb mix and shake gently until legs are coated in crumbs. Remove legs, place on baking sheet and repeat with remaining legs.

3. Pour cooking oil into a large heavy skillet to 2" depth, and heat over medium-high heat until 365°F. Add 2 or 3 pair of legs taking care not to crowd pan and fry 3-4 minutes each side or just until crust turns golden brown but meat is still very moist inside. Do not overcook or legs will be dry. Remove from oil and drain on cooling rack. Repeat with remaining legs. Arrange on platter and sprinkle with pistachio nuts and spritz with the juice of a lemon wedge.

CREOLE SPICE MIX

Ingredients:
1 tsp onion powder
1 tsp garlic powder
1 tsp paprika
½ tsp salt
1 Tbsp dried basil

1. Combine all ingredients and use as directed for Frogs' Legs. Also great for chicken or fish.

SALMON EGG MADELEINE BUTTERFLIES (304)

The alternative hors d'oeuvre I prepared for the Frogs' Legs scene was Salmon Egg Butterflies – to represent flight. Butterflies were an important motif between Will and Hannibal – transformation and metamorphosis were the Doctor's favorite topic.

Hannibal admits to Will, "With all my knowledge and intuition I could never predict you. I can feed the caterpillar, and I can whisper through the chrysalis, but what hatches follows its own nature and is beyond me."

INGREDIENTS:

24 Cornbread Madeleines (opposite)
¼ lb firm cream cheese, softened
1 small jar salmon egg caviar

Yields **12** pieces

1. Dab a spoonful of softened cream cheese on a madeleine, placing it in the middle close to one edge. Press together with a second madeleine so they hold together like two wings of a butterfly. Spoon about ½ tsp salmon eggs over the cream cheese. Set aside and repeat with remaining madeleines. Refrigerate until ready to serve.

CORNBREAD MADELEINES

Y ou need a madeleine tin – a special baking tray with small shell-shaped hollows – for making the shell-shaped wings or you can bake this batter in a mini muffin tin, split the baked muffins and fill them with cream cheese and salmon eggs. You can make the top half of the muffin into a butterfly by bisecting it and placing the left semi-circle on the right and vice versa. Press these top halves into the filling with the curved edges touching in the middle and the straight cut edges tilted up. Voila! A butterfly!

INGREDIENTS:

1 egg
3 Tbsp oil
½ cup milk
½ cup cornmeal
½ cup flour
1 tsp sugar
1 tsp baking powder
¼ tsp salt

oil and cornmeal for dusting pans

Yield 24 madeleines

1. Prepare madeleine tins by brushing shell hollows evenly with oil, making sure to get in all the grooves. Dust with cornmeal and invert to shake off excess. Set aside.

2. In a small bowl, combine egg, milk and oil. Beat well and set aside.

3. In a larger bowl, sift together flour, sugar, salt and baking powder then mix in cornmeal. Add liquid from first bowl and stir gently a few times, just until blended.

4. Pour a soupspoon of batter into each hollow of prepared madeleine tins, filling each only half full. Bake at 350°F for 6 minutes or until madeleines spring back when lightly touched. Cool slightly and remove from pan.

KHOLODETS AND ZAKOUSKI

If you think the hardest question posed in *Tome-wan* (season 2, episode 12) is "when does the hunted become the hunter" you would be wrong. The real puzzler is "What on Earth do you serve with a giant glibbery Mobius-swimming anchovy meat-jelly?"

Hannibal was scripted to serve Kholodets, a delicate aspic made from chicken. I decided zakouski, the traditional Russian tapas-style buffet, would be the perfect way to incorporate Kholodets into Hannibal's dinner for Jack.

I drew inspiration from the famous literary zakouski in "Dead Souls". Like the Chief of Police in Gogol's novel, Jack, Chief of the FBI's BSU, is presented with a table laden with a glorious assortment of Russian hors d'oeuvres: Sturgeon Head Pie, pickles, iced vodka and, of course, caviar with blini.

This opulent spread did nothing to impress Laurence Fishburne who had cast and crew howling with his Kholodets gag. Yes, he pretended to gag when he tasted it. I hesitate to relate the complicated and difficult recipe for the aspic Hannibal made, especially since anchovies and wild boar skulls have no place in a proper Kholodets, but I have adapted it into a lovely cold main course dish "Mobius Fish in Aspic" (p145) that you can serve with zakouski.

ZAKOUSKI CAVIAR PLATTER WITH BLINI (212)

To create a zakuski caviar platter, use a selection of these things: salmon egg caviar, sturgeon caviar, tobiko (flying fish eggs), smoked salmon, chopped egg salad, sour cream and pickled herring. And, as with Russian tradition, stacks of blini to spread everything on. For vegans, colourful caviar (such as CaviArt or Kelp Caviar) made by molecular spherification from fruit juices and seaweed can be purchased at specialty shops. Tomato Brains (p79) look very much like salmon egg caviar and, sprinkled with sea salt and olive oil, make an elegant addition to a caviar platter.

COCKTAIL BLINI

The large and crêpe-like type of blini, made from yeast-risen buckwheat, is more common in Russia, but I like these little bites because they are the size of silver dollars – so easy to make and so easy to eat. If you are like me and eat half the blini as they are cooking, better double the recipe if you plan to have any left for your guests. When doubling the recipe, you can use the whole egg instead of doubling the yolk.

INGREDIENTS:

½ cup milk
1 egg yolk
½ tsp honey
1 Tbsp butter melted
¼ cup all-purpose flour
3 Tbsp buckwheat flour
¼ tsp salt
½ tsp baking powder

butter for frying

Yields **24** tiny blini

1. In a medium-sized bowl, mix together flours, salt and baking powder.

2. In a small bowl, beat together milk, yolk, honey and butter. Add all at once to flour mixture and beat lightly until just combined. Let batter rest for 20 minutes.

3. Heat sauté pan over medium heat. Brush lightly with butter and pour batter a half-tablespoon at a time, forming little pancakes the size of a silver dollar. When small bubbles start to break on the surface of the pancakes (about 1½ minutes), flip them over to cook on the other side (about 1 minute). Remove from pan, wipe pan clean with paper towel and repeat until all the batter is used.

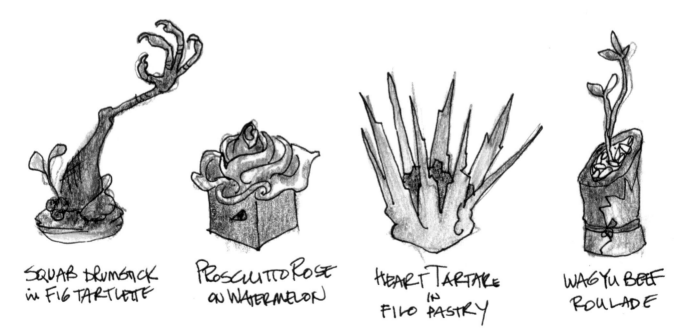

SQUAB DRUMSTICK in FIG TARTLETTE

PROSCIUTTO ROSE ON WATERMELON

HEART TARTARE in FILO PASTRY

WAGYU BEEF ROULADE

HANNIBAL'S DISARMING WAY WITH HAM

Sometimes you've got an extra arm and a lot of time on your hands. This is the case in Season 3 when Hannibal is in Florence. Happier days. "I've hardly killed anyone," he marvels to Bedelia almost disbelieving his own contentment as they gaze at the sun-kissed skyline.

Alas, no such contentment relaxing in the rosy Tuscan dawn for me! Bryan Fuller, our brilliant energetic showrunner, had just made an ALL CAPS email request for something REALLY GOOD to make from a spare arm.

"He could make it like a Peking Duck," I suggested by return email. "That's pretty tortuous: the duck is scalded, hung by the neck, blown up until its skin separates from its body…then it's brushed with hot glaze and roasted. How about Peking Arm?"

"Ummm…or cured like ham?" I upsell this next idea by describing the curing process. "The meat has all the blood drained out, it's buried in salt, then unearthed, bound up and left swinging from a meat hook in the cellar until parched and shrunken. Mummified. Then once the arm has cured, the meat gets cut off the arm in feathery slices that Hannibal spreads out to look like a pheasant wing…" I was referencing Chiyoh's prey. But I was actually remembering an elaborate Chinese appetizer my mother used to make from different kinds of meat and pickles cut into feathery shapes and arranged to look like a phoenix.

The next day, a new script came out describing Hannibal making Arm-Ham Wing then later being made into Peking Hannibal thus giving me the immeasurable pleasure of seeing my words in the scripts and on the screen.

HOME-CURED HAM

This recipe is an Ital-Canadian version of prosciutto. If you watch the ham closely as it cures and don't take any shortcuts. (Remember, you're NOT Hannibal. Only HE can cure a ham overnight with a bit of salt and a hair-dryer.) It will take several days to cure and almost a year to transform into buttery salty-sweet prosciutto. You have to monitor it closely to make sure it is curing without rot. Only try this if you have a place to hang it, ventilated but undisturbed, in cool humidity. Also helps if you have the guidance of an Italian uncle who cured his own sausages in the old country. If you do, you will be rewarded by a truly delicious prosciutto that you will be very proud to serve.

INGREDIENTS:

1 rear leg of freshly butchered pork
with ball joint attached
12-20 kilos coarse salt
a wooden box the leg will fit in easily
20 lb weight and wooden board

cayenne, paprika, ground black pepper

1. Weigh the ham so you can calculate the cure time. Make sure the central vein is well-drained of blood. You can press any blood out by pushing down on the meat with your fist. If there is any blood, it will ooze out by the ball joint where you can dab it off with paper towels. Work from the hock to the thigh and push the blood out on the large cut end.

2. In a wooden box with slab of wood that fits just inside, pour an inch of salt. Add the ham and rub well with salt, especially the exposed cut area, paying special attention to the flesh around the bone. Pour the salt around the sides of the leg and fill the box with salt burying the leg in at least one inch of salt. Place the slab of wood on top and the weight on top of the wood.

3. Let it cure in a cool place for 3 days per kilo, less a day. This will draw out all the excess liquid from the meat.

4. Remove leg from salt and wash off salt with white wine and wipe very dry. Rub all over with paprika and cayenne, mixed 50/50. Rub a generous amount over exposed cut flesh and push lots of spice mix into any crevices, especially around the bone. Use a length of rope tied around the ankle to hang the leg in a ventilated room such as a cold cellar where the conditions are consistently around 60°F, 65% humidity and there is good ventilation. Check occasionally as the leg hangs. Mould will grow but this is fine. If a hideously rank smell develops, this is rot, so you have to throw the whole thing away before the neighbours call 911, and try again next winter. After 6 months, scrape off any mould, rub black pepper onto the cut area and smear the entire surface with lard or shortening. Hang for another 3 to 10 months when it will be ready to eat. Cut off dark hard outer crust and mould, then slice prosciutto thinly. Serve with olives, bread and almonds.

GUIDE TO BUYING PATA NEGRA
AND THE CONNOISSEUR'S ULTIMATE HAM, JAMÓN IBÉRICO DE BELLOTA

I f reading the directions for making your own ham has made you exhausted but peckish, the best thing is to dash to the store and purchase a professionally cured ham. Hannibal adores Jamón Ibérico de Bellota and it is arguably the finest ham in the world. Made from happy little black-hoofed Iberian (pata negra) boars who spend their brief lives roaming under ancient oaks feasting on acorns in the Iberian sun, this delicacy was once only available in Spain. But now, it is widely exported. Sadly, they cut the iconic black hoof off at our borders to save us from succumbing to the imagined hoof and mouth pathogens that party on little pigs' toes, but all the terroir labels will be applied to let you know it is the genuine thing.

The leg ham is better than the shoulder ham but they are both excellent and the shoulder ham is smaller and less expensive.

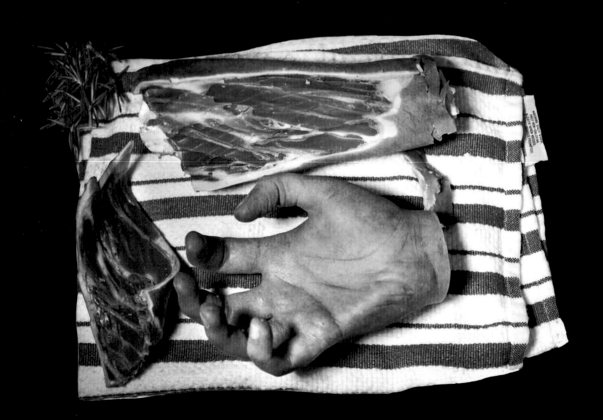

GRADES OF JAMÓN IBÉRICO

You don't have to be Michael Pitt with a bowie knife and crazy eyes to tell a good ham when you see it. Breeding, feeding and curing standards have been rigorously observed since Phoenicians first domesticated the wild Black Iberian boars on the oak-studded hills of the Spanish *dehesa*. And now that Jamón Ibérico is being widely exported and imitated, the Spanish government is tightly regulating the labelling of its most prized delicacy, so you can be assured of its authenticity.

Jamón Ibérico de Bellota are pure-bred free-range pata negra pigs who have lived their whole little lives gambolling in the ancient oak groves of Southwest Spain, fed only acorns and cured for 3-4 years or longer. It is the best you can buy.

Jamón Ibérico de Recebo or Cebo de Campo is made from cross-bred pata negra pigs that have been fed free-range on acorns with a cereal supplement and cured for 3 years. It's almost as good but doesn't have the exquisite flavour of de Bellota.

Jamón Ibérico de cebo or Jamón Ibérico are cross-bred Black Iberian boars (pata negra), not free-range, fed on cereal and cured for 2 years. All Jamón Ibérico is excellent, but this grade is not quite as meltingly marbled with fat and nutty in flavour as de Bellota or de Recebo.

Paleta Ibérico is made from the smaller front leg and not as fatty as the Jamón, made from the rump end, but is a delicious, less expensive choice.

Serrano ham is very good but not Iberian (pata negra). Made from white pigs that are not free-range and have been cereal-fed.

The ham is best enjoyed when cut freshly from the leg. Bars, restaurants and even home kitchens of Jamón Ibérico afficianados often display a whole bone-in jamón in a *jamonera* or gondola (ham holder stand) where it stays, unwrapped and unrefrigerated and always ready to serve. When you want a few slices, you simply carve them off. Pre-sliced Jamón Ibérico is available in vacuum-sealed packages but the quality suffers greatly in this form. If you have a tapas party, you could order a whole ham then leave the rest in a cool place on your kitchen counter to nibble on for the next three of four months. Or take a trip to Spain and slip into any tapas bar for a taste of Hannibal's favourite cure.

Prosciutto Melon Peacock Tail (303)

Hannibal has a few arms left over from sculpting the Murder Heart he leaves for Will, so he speed-cures one with salt and herbs, then carves the resulting ham into feathery shapes that he forms into a pheasant's wing. Lovely Bedelia serves it on a tray to a quibbling Sogliato just before a well-chilled ice pick delivers Hannibal's final point.

With much less arm-waving, you can achieve a similarly dramatic feathery presentation using fruit and prosciutto.

Ingredients:

1 small papaya
1 half cantaloupe, ripe but firm
1 kiwi fruit
strawberries
blueberries

20 slices of prosciutto

Yields appetizer platter for **8-10**

1. Cut cantaloupe into very thin wedges (about ½"). You will get 16-18 wedges out of the half cantaloupe. Lay one wedge on the cutting board and, using the sharp tip of a paring knife, cutting at a 24° angle, make many thin parallel slices from the peel out to the thin edge of the wedge, like the teeth of a comb. This will enable you to straighten out the curve of the peel side of the wedge. Repeat with all the cantaloupe wedges.

2. Cut papaya lengthwise (from stem end to blossom end) into ½" slices, keeping seeds in the centre.

3. Peel and cut kiwi into ⅛" slices.

4. Halve 4 strawberries.

5. Arrange on tray. Place 3 pairs of cantaloupe wedges on tray with peel edges back-to-back. Straighten peels to resemble a feather's spine and spread out slashed flesh on either side to resemble feathers. Place one slice of papaya at the top of each melon pair. Place kiwi slice at the base of each papaya slice and a strawberry half on kiwi. With the rest of the fruit, layer on more feathers using the same technique. Roll individual slices of prosciutto into rosettes or ruffles and place around feathers.

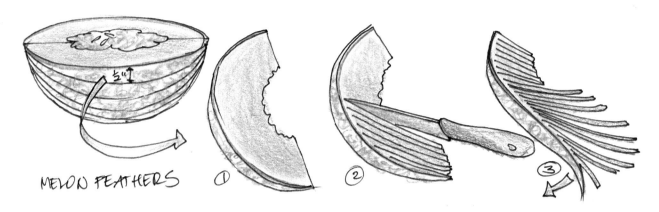

MELON FEATHERS ① ② ③

Arm Ham Wing (303)

Those of you who love a challenge may wish to replicate the wing that Hannibal made from Anthony "Scarf Dad" Dimmond's arm – a tasty little morsel he had left over from the corpse-heart valentine he left in the apse of the Norman Chapel. It was the heart that changed into a hart: the horrifyingly adorable baby Wendigo.

INGREDIENTS:

one Jamón Ibérico, bone-in

Yields appetizer or tapas for up to **40**

1. Separate the leg from the shank at the stifle joint and cut off the hoof so the shank end is about 10" long. Using a thin slicing knife, carve several long thin pieces from the leg end until the shank approximates the size and shape of a man's forearm. Place it on a tray. This will be the arm upon which you build the wing. The long shavings will be the pin feathers.

2. From the leg, carve long thin strips with a ribbon of fat on one side. You will need about 10 strips 1" wide x 5-6" long, 12 strips 1" wide x 3-4" long and and about 20 small strips about 2" long. Experiment with making smaller short V-cut strips or various types of cuts that curl like soft downy underfeathers.

3. Arrange these feathers in rows on top of the arm piece, smallest pieces at the top and larger feathers at the tip of the wing. They should stick together because of the natural oils in the ham but if you like, secure them in place with toothpicks. If you are serving more than 6, more feathers can be carved from the off-cuts and the "arm" and placed on the wing in several more layers.

4. Garnish with fruits, nuts and bread or asparagus and olives.

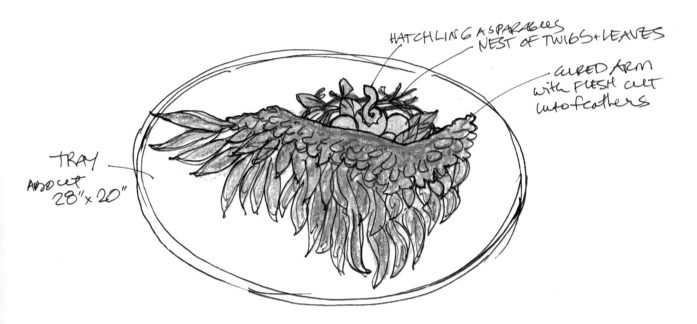

HATCHLING ASPARAGUES
NEST OF TWIGS+LEAVES

CURED ARM
with FLESH CUT
into feathers

TRAY
ALSO cut
28" x 20"

PROSCIUTTO ROSES ON WATERMELON (107)

A feast must present itself, declares Hannibal as the culture vultures flock around him at the opera, demanding invitations to dinner. Rude of them, perhaps, but Hannibal, always looking to rotate the contents of his freezer, obliges them with a feast. Drawn from the hors d'oeuvres file he keeps in his glistering stingray recipe box, here is a pretty and pleasing bite of fruit and ham.

INGREDIENTS:

12 thin slices of prosciutto
½ watermelon
stems of fresh basil tips

Yields **1** dozen hors d'oeuvres

1. Form roses: Separate prosciutto slices and lay them flat, not touching on a cookie sheet. Freeze for 15 minutes to make the slices easier to handle. Holding a slice of prosciutto on its edge, with the fatty white edge uppermost, twirl loosely in a spiral then pinch the bottom of the spiral together. With your fingertips, gently flare out the upper edge of the slice to resemble the ruffled petals of a rose. Repeat with the remaining slices.

2. Cut off the rind off the watermelon and cut melon into twelve 1¼" cubes. Place one rose on each cube. Garnish with a basil leaf. Refrigerate until ready to serve.

GALANTINE OF CHICKEN STUFFED WITH RABBIT (106)

You don't have to have Hannibal's surgical skill to bone a chicken while keeping the meat and the skin all in one piece, but it might be easier to ask your butcher to do this for you. If you relish a challenge, use a good boning knife or a very sharp paring knife and follow the steps below. For the filling, you can substitute cubes of pheasant for rabbit if you prefer. If using rabbit, don't discard the kidneys — they are a special delicacy.

INGREDIENTS:

Filling:

1 lb lean ground veal

1 rabbit, boned, cut in ½" cubes, and kidney

3 eggs

¼ tsp ground rosemary

1 tsp salt

3 cloves garlic, crushed

1 cup shelled pistachios, whole

1 cup diced carrots

½ cup bread crumbs

Roll:

one 3½ lb chicken, skin on, boned in one piece

5-7 dried figs, softened in water overnight

½ tsp rosemary

½ tsp salt

1 tsp olive oil

Yields **1** pâté

5" diameter x 12" long

FILLING:

1. In a large bowl, combine all ingredients, mix well by hand as set aside.

TO SHAPE GALANTINE:

1. Place clean dishtowel on working surface and cover with a sheet of plastic wrap. Lay chicken out flat, skin side down in the middle of the plastic wrap. Using a meat mallet, flatten the chicken into an even thickness. Spread filling over chicken in an even layer. Place figs in single file in a row from left to right. With the help of the towel, roll filled chicken up into a log. Stretching skin to cover the whole roll and using a large needle and heavy thread, stitch skin to close up the roll. Tie with butcher's string at regular intervals along the roll to hold the shape.

2. Brush roll with olive oil and sprinkle rosemary and salt over surface of roll. Transfer to roasting pan and roast at 350°F for 1 hour. Allow to rest for at least 20 minutes before slicing. Remove thread and string from slices before serving. Thick slices can be served warm, room temperature or cold as a first course or arrange thin slices on a charcuterie platter. Great with garnishes like gerkins, pickled onions, mostarda, fresh figs and crusty bread.

HOW TO BONE A CHICKEN IN ONE PIECE

1. Cut off wings between drummette and flat. Set aside flats and wingtips for another use.

2. Slice chicken back from neck to tail, cutting through skin and meat right down to backbone.

3. Holding flat of blade against the ribcage, using short feathery slices, separate meat from bone, working from the back to the side, around to the front of the bird, severing the thigh bone from the hip socket at the joint and stopping at the breastbone. Repeat on the other side.

4. Taking care to not cut through the skin, slice the breastbone away. Remove the thigh and drumstick bones by scraping the meat off the bones as you pull them out. The leg meat will turn inside-out like a sock and lay inside on the meat side. Remove the small drummette bones similarly.

PEKING DUCK HANNIBAL

Some of the most exquisite dishes call for cooking techniques that seem tantamount to torture. In anticipation of capturing Hannibal, Verger licks his malformed chops imagining his foe prepared like a Peking Duck, salivating as Cordell describes the recipe with the deadpan demeanor of an executioner.

To make Peking Duck, one must separate the skin from the body by pumping air between the skin and the subcutaneous layer of fat. Then scald the inflated bird in boiling water until the ballooned skin shrinks back. Rub it with salt and brush it with boiling honey, then let it hang by the neck to swing in a cool breeze all night. Finally, roast in a hot, hot oven until the skin is crisp and mahogany brown and the tender flesh is running with molten fat.

As we prepared for the scene, we were all deeply aware of the homage we were paying to Peter Greenaway whose brilliant 1980's film "The Cook, the Thief, His Wife and Her Lover" still inspires. The director asked me if I would like to food style directly on Mads or should he request a prosthetic Hannibal for me to dress. It was with great difficulty that I requested a dummy, but I couldn't imagine subjecting Mikkelsen to full-body make-up and being made to lie naked for hours on a table while I garlanded him with fruit and brushed him with honey. A sad sacrifice for me. But severing his prosthetic head and tossing it around the set while we prepped the oven scene sort of made up for it. Sort of…

PEKING HANNIBAL DUCK WRAPS (306)

I t's a lot of work to make a worthy Peking duck, but you can attain an almost equal yom-factor simply by purchasing one of those glistening ducks you see hanging in the windows of barbecue shops in Chinatown. It won't have the crispy melty skin of a Peking duck, but the hard work is all done for you and flavour is fantastic!

You can make or buy delicate Peking style pancake wraps for a more authentic treat but this recipe makes a heartier bite and calls for store-bought tortilla wraps. Or you can substitute frozen uncooked flaky parathas bought from an Indian or Asian grocery store and cooked according to directions on the package.

INGREDIENTS:

1 Chinese-style barbecued duck
8 flour tortilla wraps, about 6" diameter
½ cup hoisin sauce, such as
   LeeKumKee*
¼ cup melted butter or fat that has
   drained from the duck
½ red bell pepper, cut in matchstick
2 green onions, chopped
¼ English cucumber, cut in matchstick

Hoisin sauce is a sweet savory Chinese barbecue sauce made from beans, sugar and soy. It's sold in jars in Asian grocers and many large supermarkets. Korean Kalbi sauce is similar but not as strong. Substitute 1 part molasses or honey and 1 part soy sauce.

Yields **16** hors d'oeuvres
or **4** appetizers

1. Remove skin from duck and cut into julienne strips. Set aside. Remove meat from bones and shred. Discard head, neck, tail and bones or reserve for making stock.

2. Using a pastry brush, coat one side of a wrap with butter. In a sauté pan over medium-high heat, place the wrap butter-side down and fry until small brown spots begin to appear. Remove and repeat with remaining tortilla wraps.

3. Place a wrap browned side up and brush the entire surface with ½ tsp of hoisin sauce. Arrange ¼ cup duck meat and 1 Tbsp skin on lower half of wrap. Top with 1 Tbsp cucumber, 1 Tbsp red pepper and 1 tsp green onions. Fold wrap in half like a demi-lune to cover filling and brush both sides with butter. Set aside and repeat with remaining wraps.

4. Just before serving, in a sauté pan over medium-high heat, heat each filled wrap on both sides until wrap is spotted brown and a bit crispy, adding butter to the pan if necessary. Cut demi-lunes in half to make wedges and serve with extra hoisin sauce on the side.

ROASTED MARROW BONES

That most esteemed American food writer, Waverly Root wrote in the 1980s that bone marrow "is the rather mucilaginous matter which fills bones and is considered a particular delicacy by cannibals". Perhaps there were a lot of cannibals about in Victorian England when it was de rigueur for every hostess to own a set of beautifully engraved silver marrow spoons. Now, it's more fashionable to serve marrow bones canoe-cut bisecting the marrow end-to-end so you don't need special scoop-shaped spoons to burrow down to the yummy bits.

Hannibal has a few choice leg bones left over to garnish Gideon's Clay Roasted Thigh. He loves the unparalleled richness of the warm unctuous marrow. Here's what I served Mikkelsen and Izzard when they dined on Gideon's clay-wrapped thigh. After you've enjoyed the marrow, save the bones. You can use them for Bone Shooters should your elegant dinner turn into a bacchanal or wash and use as decoration to give your platters a Hannibalesque look.

INGREDIENTS:

three 4" long beef centre-cut marrow
    bones, canoe-cut
salt, pepper to taste

Yields **6** pieces or
2 appetizer-sized servings

1. To draw out all the blood, soak the marrow bones, refrigerated, in brine (1 tsp salt per cup of water) for 12-24 hours, changing the brine every 3-4 hours. I always skip this part because I like the dark brown bits on the roasted marrow.

2. Preheat oven to 400°F. Loosely crumple a sheet of aluminum foil on a cookie sheet or broiling pan and place the marrow bones, cut-side up, on the foil, pressing them into the foil to keep them from rocking about on the pan. Roast until marrow is slightly puffy, translucent and brown around the edges, and soft and hot all the way through, about 8-12 min. Test by inserting the tip of a knife into the marrow – it should be soft all the way through. Remove from tray and place on serving platter. Sprinkle with coarse sea salt and serve with Quinoa Taboule (p165) on the side.

WAGYU BEEF ROULADES (107)

Hannibal uses Wagyu beef for this hors d'oeuvre, or so says the lab report. Wagyu is intensely marbled beef that comes from specially bred Japanese cattle that have massages and enjoy beer and sake with their feed. Wagyu beef is raised in several countries but the original and most prized, such as Kobe beef, is from Japan and named after the region it comes from. Authentic Wagyu beef is very expensive, so you might want to substitute beef tenderloin in this recipe.

Rolling these is very easy if you use a bamboo mat like the ones used for making Japanese maki sushi rolls. Otherwise, use a linen towel – as in the torchon method for making foie gras (p33).

INGREDIENTS:

one ½-lb piece of Wagyu beef sirloin, or
   beef tenderloin
1 cup short grain rice for sushi
4 tsp seasoned rice wine vinegar*
¼ cup Korean BBQ sauce**
(optional) Chinese chives, blanched

12 pc parchment paper about 5" x 5"

*substitute: 1 Tbsp rice wine vinegar, 1 tsp sugar, ¼ tsp salt
**substitute: ¼ cup soy sauce, 1 T brown sugar, 2 tsp chili hot sauce, ¼ tsp crushed garlic

Yields **24** pieces

1. Place beef into freezer for 30 minutes to firm the meat so it can be sliced thinly.

2. Cook rice according to directions, cool and mix in rice wine vinegar.

3. Remove beef from freezer. It should semi frozen. Cut across grain into ⅛" slices. Gently shape and pound slices into squares 4" x 4" on the pieces of parchment paper.

4. Turn a square of beef onto sushi mat, paper side up. Peel off and discard paper. Spread a thin layer of rice on beef and roll up tightly. Tie circumference of roll in three places with a Chinese chive or butcher's string. Brush with Korean BBQ sauce. Repeat with remaining beef and rice.

5. Grill lightly just to sear beef. Cut each roll in half for hors d'oeuvre size.

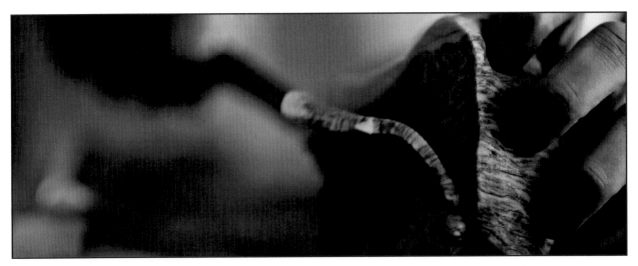

CARPACCIO (107)

Named for the blood-red paintings of renaissance artist Vittore Carpaccio, this sophisticated dish is easy to prepare: raw beef – sliced ultra-thin and garnished with olive oil, cheese and colourful condiments. The success of this dish depends entirely on using first quality ingredients.

Ask your butcher to slice the beef for carpaccio or you can do it at home by semi-freezing the beef for about 20-30 minutes - just enough to firm it. (Don't freeze it solid or your knife will never pass through). With a sharp knife, slice across the grain as thinly as possible. Thicker end bits can be pounded thinner between two sheets of plastic wrap, using a meat mallet or a rolling pin.

INGREDIENTS:

8 oz beef tenderloin, very thinly sliced

1 cup baby arugula or other baby greens

1 Tbsp olive oil

1 oz Parmesan or Crotonese cheese, shaved

sea salt and freshly grated pepper to taste

capers, onions, sun-dried tomatoes (optional garnishes)

Yields 4 servings

1. Cover the serving platter with a layer of arugula leaves and arrange the slices of beef overlapping on top. Drizzle with olive oil, top with cheese and, if you wish, a sprinkling of capers, thinly sliced red onion and/or thinly sliced sun-dried tomatoes. Sprinkle with salt and pepper and serve with warm crusty bread.

SIDE PLATTERS:

BEETLE·N·FEATHER

PESTO & TOMATO TOASTS

MEAT FLOWERS

FEATHER & BONE

MARROW PARSLEY SALAD

SEED POD of GRATED HORSERADISH

WATERMELON CARPACCIO (201)

In Season 2, Helpful Hannibal feeds Dr Chilton a delicate vegetarian dinner out of concern for the kidney he lost when Dr Abel Gideon harvested it in Season 1. This vegetarian carpaccio was a side dish to Chilton's meal of Ash-Salt Baked Celeriac.

INGREDIENTS:

1 wedge watermelon
3 oz block feta cheese
baby arugula to garnish

Drizzle:
2 Tbsp lemon juice
1 Tbsp honey
1 Tbsp olive oil

sea salt, freshly ground pepper

Yields appetizer for **4**

1. Cut a 4" slice from the middle of the wedge of watermelon. Set aside the rest for another use. Trim off and discard the rind of the mid-section piece and cut into ⅛" thick slices.

2. Cut the block of feta in half diagonally to create two triangular blocks. Cut in ⅛" slices.

3. On a platter or on individual salad plates, arrange triangles of feta and watermelon over arugula. Drizzle with lemon juice, honey and olive oil and sprinkle with salt and pepper.

MOCK ESCARGOTS À LA BOURGUIGNONNE

The first few episodes of Season 3 are alive with crawling, feasting, flaming snails. Hannibal will inform those gathered at his table that snails can be carnivorous and that, in times of food scarcity, they will cannibalize each other to survive — only to be devoured by swarms of writhing firefly larvae. Picturing this, you may feel less enthusiastic about eating them. If that happens, try these mock escargot made from mushrooms. They're what I made for Eddie Izzard who preferred them to the real snails.

INGREDIENTS:

6 to 8 large portobello mushroom caps
2 garlic cloves, crushed
1 Tbsp shallot, minced
½ cup butter
salt, pepper to taste
¼ cup red wine
2 Tbsp chopped parsley
24 escargot shells

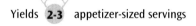

Yields **2-3** appetizer-sized servings

1. Using a biscuit cutter, cut 1" rounds out of the Portobello mushroom caps and, using a paring knife, trim each circle into a rounded comma shape. Reserve mushroom scraps and off-cuts for another use.

2. Melt 1 Tbsp of the butter in a sauté pan over medium-high heat, add garlic and shallots and sauté until softened. Add trimmed mushrooms, salt and pepper and sauté on both sides until slightly brown (about 4 minutes). Add wine and boil until it reduces by half (about 5 minutes). Stuff 1 mushroom piece into each escargot shell, twisting the "tail" of each comma shape so it resembles a snail. Arrange on individual serving dishes.

3. Add the rest of the butter and the parsley to the pan and sauté just until butter has melted and is bubbling but not browning. Pour over "snails" and serve with crusty bread.

FAUX FOIE TORCHON (105)

This is what I served to Gina Torres to stand in as duck liver during the filming of the foie gras scenes with Hannibal, Jack and Bella.

These faux foie slices do not have the silky texture and unctuous flavour of duck liver but they are yummy, versatile and vegetarian.

As a snack, top with a little salsa; as an appetizer, top with Maple Cherry Tomatoes (p76) or blanched spinach and bacon bits or melted cheese. As a light lunch, serve several slices with Ratatouille (p153). The food colouring is optional – I added it to make the slices look like foie gras.

INGREDIENTS:

4 cups vegetable stock or chicken stock
1 cup corn meal
½ tsp salt
¼ cup olive oil, butter or rendered duck fat
2 Tbsp grated Parmesan cheese

4 drops green food colouring
5 drop pink food colouring

2 large paper coffee cups

Yields **12** slices

1. Prepare moulds: Slash a large-sized paper coffee cup from top to bottom following the seam. Squeeze the top together so the top circumference is the same as the bottom, making a cylinder. Wrap with tape to secure. It will be a bit of an angle but that's OK. Repeat to make a second mould. Set aside.

2. In a heavy-bottomed saucepan over medium-high heat, bring 3½ cups of the stock to boil. Reduce heat to medium-low and slowly add corn meal in a slow stream, stirring constantly with a wire whisk. Allow mixture to bubble very gently over low heat, stirring every 5 minutes.

3. In a small cup, dissolve food colouring in the remaining ½ cup of stock then add to corn meal mixture, a spoonful at a time, until mixture is pale pinkish-tan in colour. Continue simmering and frequently stirring mixture until thickened and grains are completely softened and not gritty, about 25-35 minutes. Stir in Parmesan and butter.

4. Pour into prepared paper cups and refrigerate for at least 2 hours. When ready to serve, peel paper away from Faux Foie roll, trim off angled ends and slice into discs about ½" thick. Arrange on plates then warm in microwave for 30-40 seconds and top with Maple Cherry Tomatoes or ready-made salsa.

MAPLE CHERRY TOMATOES

INGREDIENTS:

1 pt cherry tomatoes
2 Tbsp olive oil
1 Tbsp maple syrup
salt, pepper to taste

1. Remove and discard stems and sepals from tomatoes and cut tomatoes in half. In a small baking dish, place the tomatoes together snugly, so they don't roll around, cut sides up. Drizzle maple syrup and olive oil evenly over all. Roast in oven or toaster oven preheated to 375°F for 30 minutes, or until skins are blistered. Remove and serve on Faux Foie Torchon rounds or on slices of garlic toast, sprinkled with salt and pepper.

TOMATO BRAIN BARQUETTES (107)

José Andrés, our brilliant culinary advisor told me about Tomato Brains. They are a lesson in seeing the unusual in the ordinary. If you gently tear away the flesh from a whole tomato, you will reveal the seed jelly clusters which shimmer within every tomato like handfuls of ruby cabochons – or the brains of tiny Martians, depending on how your mind works. José suggested stuffing them in pastry shells for Hannibal's grand banquet. I've added a schmeer of tapenade to add a bit of zing. You could use mustard instead of tapenade if you prefer.

INGREDIENTS:

12 puff-pastry barquettes or tartlet
   shells

3 to 4 large ripe plum tomatoes
2 Tbsp prepared tapenade or chopped
   Niçoise or Kalamata olive
freshly ground pepper and sea salt
chervil, parsley or chive

To make 24 Pastry Shells:
one 14 oz pkg frozen puff pastry
¼ cup melted butter, optional

1. Cut off the top ½" of the stem end of a tomato. Leaving the seed jelly clusters intact, gently tear away the tomato flesh to reveal a wedge-shaped cluster of seeds. Slide the tip of a sharp paring knife under the seed cluster to release it from the core of the tomato. Carefully set aside on a plate. Repeat until you have 12 to 16 clusters. Reserve the tomato flesh for use at another time.

2. Spread ½ tsp of tapenade in the bottom of 12 of the prepared pastry shells, Slide one or two tomato brains in to shell. Season with salt and pepper. Garnish with a leaf of chervil, parsley or lengths of chive.

TO MAKE 24 PASTRY SHELLS:

1. Thaw dough according to instructions. On floured board, roll half of the dough to ⅛" thickness into a rectangle that is about 9" x 7". Press into small barquette tins or shape shells as follows: Cut dough into rounds using a 2" diameter cookie cutter. Using a 1" diameter cutter, press an impression in the middle of each 2" round. The impression should be deep but not cut all the way through the dough. Prick inside round with fork tines. Repeat with remaining dough.

2. Place rounds on baking sheet. In an oven pre-heat to 400°F, bake for 12-15 minutes or until golden brown. Set aside to cool as you prepare fillings.

3. Hollow out the rounds for filling by pulling out a few layers of the center round from each, leaving a layer on the bottom and ¼" wall around the outer circumference of each shell, thus forming a well for the fillings.

4. Brush shells with butter for flavor, if desired.

HAVING FRIENDS
FOR DINNER

MAINS - MEAT

LUNG AND LOIN IN WINE SAUCE (101)

To paraphrase Mrs Beeton, "First, get a lung". Easier said than done since lung is not legally sold in many jurisdictions. Once you get it, prepare the lung for cooking by soaking it, cubed, in salt-water overnight in the fridge. The next day, put an Egyptian cotton apron over your bespoke white dress shirt then drain the lungs and, with your bare hands, squeeze out the water gently but persuasively – urgently, even…

If you can't get lung, double the amount of tenderloin and you will have a truly delectable Beef Bourguignonne. For the stock, home-made beef or veal stock made from roasted bones is best, but reconstituted beef stock concentrate works fine.

INGREDIENTS:

For the wine sauce:
4 Tbsp butter
2 cloves garlic, minced
¼ cup flour
2 cups red wine
2 cups beef stock
salt, pepper to taste

For the lung and loin:
4 Tbsp olive oil
1 lb veal lungs, trimmed of tracheal
  tubes and cut in 1" cubes
1 lb beef tenderloin, cut in 1" cubes
2 cups Portobello mushrooms, trimmed
  and cut in ½" slices
1 cup baby red onions, peeled and
  par-boiled
2 cups baby carrots, par-boiled

Yields **4** main course servings

1. In a large deep frying pan, heat butter over medium heat. Add garlic and sauté until light golden brown. Add flour and stir constantly until golden brown.

2. Stir in wine and stock, whisking to smooth out any lumps and cook, whisking frequently, until thickened. Remove from heat and set aside.

3. In a large sauté pan, heat 2 tsp olive oil over high heat. Season beef with salt and pepper, add to pan and sauté til medium rare. Remove from pan. Wipe pan dry with paper towel and return to heat with 2 tsp olive oil. Add lung and brown, stirring constantly til slightly browned but not releasing too much liquid. Remove from pan. Wipe pan dry and return to heat. Add 2 tsp olive oil and half of the mushrooms. Sauté until mushrooms brown and begin to release moisture. Remove from pan and repeat with remaining mushrooms.

4. Return wine sauce to heat and bring to boil. Add pearl onions and carrots and simmer til tender. Add lungs, beef and mushrooms and simmer just til heated through but beef still medium-rare. Remove to serving dish and serve with herbed rice, noodles or buttery mashed potatoes.

DINUGUAN OR "CHOCOLATE" STEW WITH PUTO

This classic dish of the Philippines makes use of lungs, liver and blood, Hannibal's favourite ingredients. It is full of rich tangy flavour. You can find fresh or frozen pork blood at South American sausage-makers or at Asian supermarkets. For this recipe, the blood should be raw (fresh or frozen). The cooked blocks of blood in Chinese shops will not work. When you use the blood, whisk it thoroughly before using to smooth any blobby bits and, if you wish, pour through a strainer to be sure.

Hannibal hasn't had a chance to make this dish for his guests yet, but if you catch a glimpse of him on the streets of Manilla, hide the children!

INGREDIENTS:

¼ lb pork or beef lung, cut in ½" cube

½ lb pork liver, cut in ½" cube

1 lb pork butt, cut in 1" cube

3 Tbsp fish sauce*

1 small head garlic, peeled and minced

2 bay leaves

3 to 4 chili peppers, seeded and chopped

3 Tbsp oil

1 onion, diced

1 Tbsp sugar

salt and pepper to taste

½ cup vinegar

1 cup pork blood

Fish sauce is an anchovy-based sauce used primarily in Asian cuisine and adds a lot of flavor depth to savory dishes and dips. Buy the brands that are labeled with certified appellation of Phu Quoc. Substitute: 2 parts light soy sauce and 1 part Worchestershire sauce.

Yields **6** servings

1. In a pot, cover pork with water and simmer for 30 min. Skim off any white foam and strain. Set aside pork and reserve stock.

2. In a casserole or heavy pan, heat oil over medium-high and sauté garlic and onions until translucent. Add lung, liver, pork, bay leaves, salt and pepper and sauté for 5 minutes or til lightly browned. Add fish sauce, vinegar and bring to boil. Lower heat and simmer until most of liquid has evaporated. Add reserved stock plus enough water to make 2 cups and simmer for 5 minutes. Add blood, sugar and peppers and simmer gently for 10 minutes, until sauce thickens, stirring frequently to prevent curdling. Serve with steamed Jasmine rice, black vinegar, hot chili sauce and Puto (opposite).

PUTO

Tiny steamed cakes called Puto are the traditional accompaniment to Dinguan. Here an easy version that is dense and rich and uses regular flour instead of rice flour. When shopping for canned coconut milk, there may be a baffling number of different brands to choose from. Check the label for coconut oil content. The best brands have the higher fat content.

INGREDIENTS:

1¼ cups coconut milk
2 cups flour
¼ cup sugar
1 Tbsp baking powder
½ tsp salt

Yields **1** dozen little buns

1. Sift flour, baking powder and salt into a mixing bowl and stir to blend well. Pour in coconut milk all at once and stir together until it forms a ball. Turn ball out onto floured surface and knead very lightly a few times until smooth. Form into a long roll and cut roll into 12 equal pieces. Form each piece into a ball and place into a paper muffin cup.

2. Arrange cups in the top of a steamer, cover and steam for 5-6 minutes over rapidly boiling water. Do not overcook or the cakes will be dry.

TANDOORI LIVER (101)

Hannibal loves his — well, other people's liver. This was one of the first things I prepared for Mads Mikkelsen to eat on camera and, not yet knowing his tastes, I used pieces of pink mortadella carved to look like liver. He was disappointed it wasn't the real thing — heart and lung were also on the list of food scenes to shoot that day and he had been curious about trying them all. It was the beginning of a long list of oddities I cooked that Mads avidly sampled over the years of filming the series.

This dish is sensational served with Saffron Risotto (p175) or buttery mashed potatoes and a cooling dollop of citrusy yoghurt. Its simple preparation depends on the heavy coating of spices. Tandoori spice mix is a blend of spices including coriander, cumin, ginger, paprika, cayenne, sugar and salt. It comes already blended and can be bought by the jar in South Asian food shops. Smoked paprika, hot or sweet, can substitute for Tandoori spice mix. For extra flavour layers, garnish with bits of bacon and slow-cooked onion slices. Crisp-fried onions and garlic are great to sprinkle on dishes like this. They are sold by the bag in Indian food shops so look for them when you are picking up your Tandoori spice mix.

INGREDIENTS:

1 lb sliced liver, veal or pork

2 Tbsp Tandoori spice mix or smoked paprika

3 Tbsp butter

salt, pepper to taste

Yields **4** main-course servings

1. Dredge liver in spice mix, coating both sides heavily. Heat sauté pan over medium-high heat. Add 1 Tbsp of the butter. When butter is bubbling, add liver slices to the pan and fry for 1 minute, turn and fry other side for an additional 2 minutes, or until liver is medium-rare. Remove from pan to a covered warm platter. With a paper towel, wipe sauté pan clean of any burned spices and repeat with remaining slices.

2. When all liver slices have been cooked, arrange on serving platter, garnish with bacon and fried onion if desired and serve with Marmalade Yoghurt (below) on the side.

MARMALADE YOGHURT

This flavourful yogurt is great with Tandoori Liver. Serve it with curries too.

INGREDIENTS:

2 Tbsp orange marmalade

1 Tbsp lime juice

½ cup plain yoghurt

1. Combine marmalade, juice and yoghurt in a small bowl. Refrigerate until ready to serve.

Heart with Sausage Stuffing (101)

The heart is a splendid muscle — hard-working, lean, and low-fat. Because of this, it must be cooked one of two ways: long-cooked over gentle heat til fork-tender, or seared quickly and fiercely then served pink and rare. This recipe is for the former. To stuff it, you have to cut the heartstrings. Yes, that's what those thin connective threads are really called.

In episode 1 of the first season, we learn that Hannibal's secretary lost her heart to someone in the UK. Or maybe it was You Know Who.

If you don't have a braising pan with lid, you can use any baking pan and cover tightly with foil in lieu of lid.

INGREDIENTS:

2 pork hearts
4-6 slices bacon
salt and pepper to taste

For stuffing:
2 large honey-garlic breakfast sausages
   (about 3 oz)
½ cup herbed salad croutons, slightly
   crushed

For braising:
1 onion, rough chopped
2 carrots, rough chopped
1 cup apple cider

Yields **2** servings

1. Prepare hearts by removing large veins, rinsing chambers well and slicing through walls and heartstrings to open chambers for stuffing. Sprinkle liberally inside and out with salt and pepper. Set aside.

2. Prepare stuffing: Remove skins from sausages. Discard skins and place meat in a small bowl. Add croutons and mix well.

3. Place one heart on working surface and layer on half of the stuffing. Push stuffing into cavities well until heart is plump and overflowing. Close heart back up into approximate heart shape – no need to fully enclose stuffing. Wrap with bacon and tie together with several lengths of twine to retain shape. Repeat with remaining heart.

4. Place hearts in braising pan. Add apple cider, carrots and onion. Cover with lid or foil and roast for 45 minutes in an oven preheat to 325°F. Add water periodically to keep pan from drying out. Check degree of done-ness: juice should run pink when heart is pierced. Remove lid and roast for an additional 15 minutes to brown bacon. Juice will run clear with a trace of pink when cooked. Serve on a big pile of mashed potatoes with Aji Sauce (p88).

AJÍ SAUCE (206)

As Hannibal recovers from a murderous attack instigated by Will, Alana helps him make dinner. It's Grilled Heart. The cut up heart has been marinating in ají sauce and as Alana slides morsels of it onto barbecue sticks, he tells her, "My heart feels skewered."

This tangy sweet-hot sauce was used by Hannibal as a barbecue marinade but it is also a perfect complement for Heart with Sausage Stuffing. He made it with aji peppers puréed with yellow bell peppers to keep its golden hue. You can roast a combination of red, orange and yellow bell peppers or, to save time, buy pre-roasted red bell peppers from the deli section of your supermarket. The heat comes from ají amarillo sauce which is a purée of hot yellow peppers central to Andean cuisine since time immemorial and can be bought by the jar in Mexican or South American food shops. Add a little or a lot, depending on how fiery you like your food.

INGREDIENTS:

4 yellow, orange or red bell peppers
1 Tbsp butter
2 small shallots, peeled and chopped
½ tsp sugar
2 Tbsp white wine vinegar
1-3 tsp ají amarillo pepper sauce
salt to taste

Yields **1** cup sauce

1. Blacken the bell peppers: Roast under broiler or over medium-high barbecue, turning frequently, until skin blackens and blisters, about 15-20 minutes. Transfer to a plastic or paper bag and close tightly. Allow peppers to steam in their own heat for about 30 minutes. Remove from bag and peel off and discard skin. Remove and discard stems and seeds and dice peppers roughly. Set aside.

2. In a sauté pan over medium heat, add butter, shallots and chopped peppers and fry until translucent and soft. Lower heat and add vinegar, sugar. Simmer for 10 minutes. Transfer to food processer and process until smooth. Add aji sauce and salt to taste.

BEVERLY STEAK AND KIDNEY PIE (205)

The appearance of this pie marked a very sad day on set. Sassy Science lost Beverly, their best, most clever crime lab lass. It was the day we realized that no one was safe. If Hannibal could kill Beverly, he would kill anyone. She didn't deserve to be sliced, splayed and displayed like a Damien Hirst cow.

Although, I suppose Hannibal has a point…it is awfully rude to break into someone's home and rifle through their basement stash of body parts.

In order that forensic scientists everywhere can continue their good work, this recipe calls for beef kidneys rather than Bev kidneys. If you find their flavour too strong, use pork kidneys, which are mild and tender. Although some recipes recommend soaking kidneys in acidulated salted water, it's not necessary. Cooking completely gets rid of the faintly "kidney" smell. Trim the white out of the middle of beef kidneys because although some of it is yummy fat, much of it is gristle. Pork kidneys don't need to have their inside fat removed.

INGREDIENTS:

½ onion cut into eight wedges

1½ cups mushrooms, quartered

3 Tbsp olive oil

½ lb steak such as strip loin or rib eye, cut in ¾" cubes

½ lb beef kidney, cut into lobes then cut in ½" slices

¼ cup red wine

For gravy:

2 Tbsp butter

2 Tbsp flour

1 cup beef stock

1½ tsp Worchestershire sauce

salt, pepper to taste

1 recipe Lemon Olive Oil Pastry (p116)

Yields **1** large pie or **2** individual pies

1. In a sauté pan over medium heat, fry 1 Tbsp oil and onions, stirring occasionally. When onions begin to turn translucent, add mushrooms and cook until mushrooms begin to release their juices. Remove to medium-sized bowl and return pan to heat.

2. Increase heat to medium-high and add 1 Tbsp oil to pan. Add steak cubes and fry until steak has browned but is still pink inside, about 4 minutes. Remove to bowl of cooked mushrooms. Using a rubber spatula, scrape everything from the pan into the bowl and return pan to heat. Add the rest of the olive oil and the kidney slices. Sauté until browned but still pink then transfer to bowl of steak and mushrooms. Deglaze pan by adding wine and scraping bits off the bottom of the pan as the wine gently boils. Add pan juices to the bowl of cooked meats.

3. Reduce heat to medium, wipe pan dry and return to heat. Make a roux by adding butter and flour to the pan and stirring constantly until flour turns golden brown. Remove pan from heat. Pour juices from the bowl of meats into a measuring cup, add enough stock to make 1½ cups liquid. Add slowly to the roux, stirring constantly. Return to heat and stir constantly as gravy thickens. Add to bowl of meats and stir to combine. Add Worchestershire sauce and salt and pepper to taste. Refrigerate until ready to assemble the pies.

4. Assemble the pies as for Deerly Beloved Meat Pies (p115). Or, if you want to make them with Will's bite mask, as Hannibal does for his Beverly Kidney Pie, follow the directions on the next page.

TO MAKE THE "BITE MASK" PIES:

INGREDIENTS:

1 batch of Lemon Olive Oil Pastry into 4
    equal pieces
4 individual-sized foil pie pans

Yields **2** individual pies

1. To make the mask tops, take one foil pie pan and press it down, inverted, over an upside-down bowl so the flat bottom of the foil is pushed out to curve like a dome. Keeping the lip of the foil pan flat, place it on the cookie sheet, dome side up. Roll out one of the pastry quarters into a 7" diameter circle and using the bottom of a funnel or the lid of a pen as a cutter, make a small hole in the centre of the pastry circle. Cut 5 more holes around the centre hole to represent the air holes of the bite mask. At the top third of the circle, draw a shallow "w" with your knife tip, and remove the pastry above the W. Lift the resulting pastry shape onto the dome of the reshaped foil pie pan and trim the circle of dough so it falls just to the rim of the foil pan. Reserve the pastry scraps. Repeat with another foil pan and another quarter of dough and place the pastry-covered foil domes on a cookie sheet.

2. To make the bottom shells, add half of the pastry scraps to a quarter piece of the pastry dough and roll into an 8" diameter circle. Using a fork, poke holes in the entire surface of the pastry circle. Carefully slide the pastry circle over a foil pie pan. Fit another foil pie pan on top of it, snugly sandwiching the pastry between the two pans. Trim off excess pastry and place on a cookie sheet beside mask tops. Repeat with the last piece of dough. Place on cookie sheet.

3. Bake at 400°F for 12–15 minutes or until pastry is golden brown, removing the top foil pans at 8 minutes to allow the bottom shells to brown. Cool completely before handling.

4. When ready to serve, heat filling and set aside. Lift pastry bottom shells off the foil pans, place each on a dinner plate, fill with heated beef and kidney filling, place a pastry mask on top of each and serve to much applause!

PINHEAD PORK BELLY WITH SUGAR CANE SKEWERS

G ideon's roasted leg from first episode of Season 3 was inspired by Pinhead and in turn inspired this recipe for slow-cooked pork belly glazed in orange juice and served as a Korean Bossam lettuce wrap.

INGREDIENTS:

1 large slab pork belly (about 2½ lb)
6-8 cloves garlic
2 tsp soy sauce
1 can orange juice concentrate (10 oz)
1 cup stock
15-20 skewers cut from fresh sugar cane
   (optional)

For lettuce wrap
15-20 leaves lettuce
1½ cup cooked sticky rice, formed into
   1-inch balls
¼ cup sriracha sauce

Serves **4-6** as a small plate or tapas

1. Place pork belly, skin side down, in a large saucepan, and cover with cold water. Bring to boil on medium heat. Reduce heat and simmer, covered, for 2 hours. Drain and cool pork. Strain and reserve liquid to use as stock at another time.

2. Using a sharp knife, skin side up, make slashes in the skin of the pork belly in a 1-inch grid. Rub garlic and soy sauce into the slashes. Skewer a length of sugar cane into the centre of each square. If the skin is hard to pierce with the sugar cane, make a small incision with a paring knife first, then poke in the sugar cane skewer. Place in baking pan and pour on orange juice concentrate and stock. Cover loosely with foil. Roast at 300°F for 30 – 45 minutes or until fork-tender, adding more stock to keep pork half submerged.

3. Transfer pork to serving platter and slice into cubes along the score marks. Serve with lettuce, rice balls and sriracha sauce.

4. To eat, dab a bit of sriracha sauce on a leaf of lettuce, pick up one cube of pork belly using the skewer and place on lettuce. Pull out skewer and discard. Add one rice ball and fold lettuce over. Eat with your fingers.

TÊTE DE VEAU WITH SAUCE VERTE (113)

Complicated to prepare at home, Tête de Veau (Calf's Head) can be found in every other corner boucherie in Paris. But we are not in Paris, Toto, so here is a recipe for those of you who long to replicate the meal that Hannibal makes when we first meet the indomitable Dr Bedelia DuMaurier.

As we watch them dine together, matching wits over rolled tête, we fear it's Abigail in Hannibal's cooker and watch in horror as he and Bedelia chew through slice after slice.

Ask your butcher to bisect, bone and skin the calf's head, removing all the fat and hair and the eyes. If you have the kind of butcher who is kind and gifted enough to do all that for you then surely, he is the type of merchant who will let you buy just half. I hope so, because you are not likely to want to eat a whole head. You will use the half-tongue in the Tête de Veau and you can serve the half-brain on top gently poached or breaded and pan-fried in butter. Or freeze the brain and save it for Protein Scramble (p16) or Tortilla Sacromonte (p22) another day.

INGREDIENTS:

1 half calf's head, skinned and boned
   with tongue and brain separate
4 carrots, cut in 2" lengths
2 leeks, cut in 2" lengths
2 ribs celery, cut in 2" lengths
1 onion, quartered
1 Tbsp pickling spice mix
sea salt

Sauce Verte

1 cup parsley, flat leaf
¼ cup fresh dill weed
½ cup chopped chives
1 clove garlic, minced
1 anchovy filet
3 Tbsp capers
1 Tbsp juice from caper jar
1 Tbsp lemon juice
½ cup olive oil
salt, pepper to taste

Yields 4 servings

1. Roll the meat snugly around the tongue and tie securely with butcher's string into a 4"-5" diameter roll. If you can get large diameter meat netting from your butcher, use it to keep the calf's head in a tight neat roll. Butchers use an apparatus to stretch the netting out but rather than struggle with this, I just cut open the tube of netting so it becomes a flat rectangle, then lace the cut sides back together with butcher's twine, slide the rolled meat in and pull the laced twine so the netting tightens around the rolled meat like a corset. Or hockey skate, depending on your experience.

2. Cover with cold water in a large pot. Add carrots, leeks, celery, onion and pickling spice. Bring to boil over medium-high heat then reduce heat to low and skim off coagulated foam that rises to the top. Simmer for 5 hours. Remove from heat and drain. Check the roll all over and trim off remaining hairs or bristles. Chill until completely cool before slicing. Just before serving, cut in 1" thick slices, reheat by microwaving, covered or by sautéing in a lightly oiled frypan. Sprinkle with sea salt and serve with Sauce Verte.

SAUCE VERTE

1. Combine parsley, chives, capers, garlic, anchovy, lemon juice and caper juice in a food processor and pulse until finely chopped. With motor running, add olive oil and process until well combined. Add salt and pepper to taste.

CHEF'S CHEEKS AU POIVRE (307)

W orking in film is very collaborative. No one toils alone – even if it feels like it. I was lucky to have the help and support of a small but mighty team of talented assistants. John Kruusi was our super-shopper, grill master and mixologist (believe me, every department needs cocktails). He is a wonderful cook, very talented on the grill and has an encyclopedic knowledge of, well, everything. This is his fantastic recipe for beef cheeks – so appropriate for the scene in *Digestivo*, episode 7 of Season 3 where a very proud Hannibal watches as Will takes a big bite out of Chef Cordell's cheek. He spits it out but I'm pretty sure if John had cooked it, Will would have swallowed it and licked the plate. Here's his easy but impressive recipe for beef cheeks.

INGREDIENTS:

4 beef cheeks (approximately 2 lb)
3 Tbsp Dijon mustard
2 Tbsp butter
2 Tbsp olive oil
2 cups red wine
2 large shallots, roughly chopped
1 bay leaf
salt and pepper, to taste
one 1 oz tin green peppercorns in
    brine, drained
⅔ cup whipping cream

Yields **4** servings

1. Coat the beef cheeks generously with 2-3 Tbsp of the mustard, and season with salt and pepper.

2. In a Dutch oven or other heavy-bottomed oven-proof pot with lid, heat the butter and oil over medium-high heat. Working in batches to avoid overcrowding the pot, brown the beef cheeks on all sides. Place the beef cheeks aside on a plate. Turn the heat down to low and add the shallots and red wine, and using a wooden spoon, scrape the brown bits from the bottom of the pot.

3. Return the beef cheeks to the pot with any juices that have run out onto the plate. Add the bay leaf, cover with a lid and place in an oven preheated to 300°F. Cook for approximately 3½ hours or until the cheeks are fork-tender and look as if they are about to fall apart. If the beef cheeks are large or sinewy, this can take up to 7 hours. Remove the beef cheeks from the pot and place on a plate, covered with foil to keep warm. If you're making things ahead of time, at this point, you can separate the beef cheeks and the liquid left behind in the pot and refrigerate for a day or so. When ready to serve, re-heat the beef cheeks and rewarm the cooking liquid, adding the rest of the sauce ingredients as instructed in Step 4.

4. Return the pot to the stovetop and over low heat, whisk in the remaining 1 Tbsp of Dijon mustard, whipping cream and green peppercorns. Season with salt and pepper to taste. Serve the beef cheeks with the sauce poured over top.

PIGTAILS GANGNAM-STYLE (306)

Pigtails are so uncool, they're hot! Formerly found only in the kitchens of America's deep South, the West Indies and rural China, pigtails have been rediscovered by Nose-to-Tail chefs like Fergus Henderson, Thomas Keller and Anthony Bourdain. They are, as Mason Verger says, "mostly skin and bones" but the flavour and texture are wonderful. Par-boiling removes the excess fat and you are left with nourishing collagen-rich skin and tendons.

Cordell creates a meal to show Verger the many ways he would cook up Hannibal bit by bit, pigtails standing in for fingers. In this recipe, he cooks the tails until tender and finishes them in a Korean miso and chili sauce for a sweet-hot-salty taste sensation!

INGREDIENTS:

3 lb pig tails, chopped in 1½-inch lengths

6 Tbsp Korean fermented soy bean paste like Haechandel

4 Tbsp Korean chili paste, like Haechandel

3 Tbsp sugar

2 Tbp sesame oil (optional)

4-6 cloves garlic, crushed

2 large carrots, sliced ¼-inch into rounds

⅛ cabbage, sliced in ¼-inch shreds

Serves 4 as main course

1. Rinse pigtails well. Cover with cold water in a large saucepan, bring to boil over high heat then reduce heat and simmer for 20 minutes. Discard water and rinse pigtails. Remove any hairs or bristles. They should come out easily after the par-boiling. Clean saucepan completely, add pigtails and cover with cold water. Bring to boil over high heat then reduce heat to low and simmer for 1½ hours or until skin can be easily pieced with a fork and meat is tender.

2. In a medium-sized baking dish, combine soy bean paste, chili paste, garlic, sugar, oil and a half-cup of cooking liquid from the pigtails. Stir until well-blended. Drain pigtails (cooking liquid can be reserved and used for stock at another time). Add pigtails, carrots and cabbage and toss until all are evenly coated. Cover baking dish tightly with foil. Roast at 275°F for 45 minutes and serve with steamed rice or Siam Wookie Balls (p174).

HONG KONG RIBS (306)

For Verger's dinner, Cordell methodically bastes a roasted rack of ribs as he explains how he will cook the various parts of Dr Lecter. To shoot the scene, I used baby back ribs because they can be twisted to resemble a human ribcage. This recipe uses three prepared Chinese sauces that are sold by the jar in Asian grocery stores but you can get them at most supermarkets.

INGREDIENTS:

1 strip pork baby back ribs, about 2½ lb

2 Tbsp oyster sauce*
2 Tbsp hoi sin sauce**
2 Tbsp chili bean sauce***
2 Tbsp honey
2 Tbsp balsamic vinegar
1 Tbsp lemon juice

1 onion, quartered
3 carrots, cut in 3" lengths
2 potatoes, quartered

Oyster sauce is a thick brown sauce flavoured with oysters. Substitute 1 part soy sauce, and 1 part fish sauce or crushed anchovy, ½ part sugar.
**Hoy sin sauce is Chinese barbecue sauce. Substitute 1 part honey and 1 part miso paste.*
***Chili bean sauce is a prepared mixture of hot chili peppers, oil and bean paste. Substitute 2 parts sriracha sauce and 1 part miso sauce.*

Yields **2** main course servings

1. In a large bowl, combine hoi sin, chili bean sauce, oyster sauce, vinegar, honey and lemon juice and mix thoroughly. Remove ¼ cup of the mixture and reserve, refrigerated. Cut rib strip in two or three pieces so it will fit in your roasting pan in one layer, and add to the bowl, brushing mixture over all. Transfer ribs and marinade into an extra-large plastic zippered freezer bag, zip almost closed and press out as much air as possible. Zip completely closed and allow to marinate in refrigerator for 2 days, turning bag occasionally to make sure the ribs are marinated on all sides.

2. In the bottom of a roasting pan, spread onions, potatoes and carrots and pour in 1 cup of water. Remove ribs from plastic bag and place on top of vegetables in roasting pan. The ribs should sit above the water line. Cover snugly with foil and bake for 1½ hour in oven preheat to 300°F. Add water if necessary to keep vegetables partially submerged. Remove Ribs from roasting pan and set vegetables aside.

3. Brush reserved marinade on ribs and brown on preheated barbecue grill or under broiler for 2 minutes on each side, just enough to brown the glaze. As an accompaniment, vegetables from the roasting pan can be drained and brushed with butter. Remove to platter and serve.

LOMO SALTADO (210)

Bonding in the kitchen, Hannibal and Will cook Lomo Saltado together. Part of Will's deception is pretending he has brought a choice cut from redhead Freddie Lound's leg. Hannibal instructs, "Cut the ginger" and it became a favorite phrase to which the only reply is, "I already have."

Lomo Saltado is a popular "Chifa" dish that resulted from Chinese migrants working the mines of Peru. It's a blend of Asian and Peruvian flavours and ingredients... a hot-pepper stir-fry served on Asian rice and South American potatoes. In a culture mash-up, you can't go wrong with double carbs. For the potatoes, I like curly spicy fries for the way they echo Freddie's curly mane.

For the shoot, I used pork but in this recipe, I've used beef because it's authentic to Peruvian tradition. You can substitute chicken strips or Portobello mushrooms for the beef if you prefer.

INGREDIENTS:

12 oz sirloin steak cut in strips ¼" x ¼" x 2"
3 Tbsp white wine vinegar
1 tsp soy sauce
1 tsp Worcestershire sauce
1 to 2 cloves garlic, crushed
1 tsp grated fresh ginger, optional
½ tsp crushed cumin seeds, optional
3 Tbsp oil
½ red onion, sliced
2 plum tomatoes, in thin wedges
1 Tbsp aji sauce* or other hot pepper sauce
salt and pepper to taste
1 cup frozen spicy French fried potatoes
2-3 sprigs cilantro, chopped

*Aji sauce is a very hot sauce made from yellow aji peppers, tomatillos, cilantro and lime. Can be bought at South American or Mexican grocery stores. Substitute hot chili oil or sauce and lime juice.

Yields **4** servings

1. In a small bowl, mix vinegar, soy, Worcestershire, garlic, ginger and cumin. Add steak strips and let marinate for at least 30 minutes.

2. Heat Spicy Fries in oven as per instructions on the bag. Keep warm in oven.

3. Heat a large sauté pan or wok over high until very hot. Add 1 Tbsp oil and onions. Stir-fry on high heat until onion slices have browned in places and are turning translucent. Do not overcook – they should still be slightly crunchy. Transfer onions to bowl and set aside. Return pan to heat and add 1 Tbsp oil and half of the beef slices. Do not crowd the pan or beef will not brown. Stir-fry for 2-4 minutes or until beef has browned but still medium-rare. Transfer cooked beef to bowl of fried onions and repeat with remaining oil and beef. Wipe pan clean with paper towel and return pan to heat. Add tomatoes and aji sauce to hot pan and stir-fry until skin starts to peel away and tomatoes start to release their juices. Add beef and onions back into the pan and mix well until heated through. Add hot French fries and toss until everything is well coated with the juices. Add salt and pepper to taste.

4. Serve over steamed rice. Sprinkle with cilantro.

SILVER TONGUE DEVILS (106)

While speaking of "chatty lambs" losing their tongues, Hannibal treats Dr Chilton and Alana to an elegant dinner of Langue d'agneau en papillotte with duxelle sauce and oyster mushrooms. Enjoying the moment, he just can't resist telling them, "It's nice to have an old friend for dinner."

It's a little tricky to get lamb tongues so I'm giving you a recipe using cooked beef tongue which you can buy by the pound at a deli (Or brine and poach a fresh one yourself.)

For *Hannibal*, I folded origami lotuses out of parchment paper to present the tongues but a true "en papillotte" fully encloses its ingredients so they gently roast in their own fragrant steam. The packets are traditionally folded out of heart-shaped parchment, but this foil version is dead simple to make.

INGREDIENTS:

For the Duxelles
½ cup chopped red onions
2 cups chopped mushrooms, such as
    button or Crimini
3 Tbsp butter
½ cup white wine
¼ tsp balsamic vinegar
salt and pepper to taste

For the Tongue packets
12 oz cooked tongue, sliced ¼" thick cut
    in pieces 3" x 2"
2 tomatoes, cut in ½" dice
¼ cup white wine
4 sprigs fresh rosemary
olive oil for brushing
4 sheets light aluminum foil cut in 12"
    diameter circles

Yields **4** portions

1. Make the Duxelles: In a very large sauté pan over medium high heat, melt butter and add onions, frying until they begin to soften. Add the chopped mushrooms and sauté, stirring frequently, just until mushrooms release their juices. Add wine and boil until liquid is reduced by half. Season with salt, pepper and balsamic. Set aside to cool.

2. To make the packets, place a circle of foil on working surface. In the centre of the lower half of the circle of foil, place 1 slice of tongue, top with 1 Tbsp Duxelle, another slice of tongue and more Duxelle. Add another layer if your tongue slices are small. Sprinkle with a quarter of the diced tomato, pour 1 Tbsp wine over all and top with a sprig of rosemary. Repeat 3 times with the remaining foil and ingredients.

3. Close up the packets: Bring the upper half of the circle of foil over so the upper and lower circumferences meet. Crimp the edges together well, making the seal as airtight as possible and taking care to leave at least one inch of space all around the tongue. This is where the aromatic steam will build up during the baking, puffing out your foil packets. Repeat with remaining foil sheets. Refrigerate until 30 minutes before serving. Reserve remaining Duxelles to serve on the side.

4. Twenty minutes before serving time, place the foil packets on a baking sheet and bake in a pre-heated oven at 350° for 15 minutes. Reheat Duxelles and transfer to serving dish. Plate the foil packets unopened. When guests open their packets at the table, a lovely puff of rosemary-scented steam will rise to whet their appetites.

KIBBEH TONGUES (106)

When preparing for this scene in *Entrée*, I didn't want Caroline, Raul nor Mads to endure chewing on endless resets of cold rubbery lamb tongues that the two pages of scripted dialogue would require. In any case, lamb tongues are not really a food stylist's delight – they look like giant mauve larvae. So to get the look of plump children's tongues that I wanted, I shaped each one individually out of a bulgar mixture that I tinted with pink food colouring, then cooked in the steamer. Its nubby texture mimicked exactly the papillae-covered surface of a tongue.

The mixture I used to make the tongues is a dough used to make a wonderful Lebanese dumpling called Kibbeh. I didn't use a filling in the tongues for the shoot in order to simplify resetting, but here, I've included the meat filling of a traditional Kibbeh. Delicious served with yogurt or tzaziki or just spritzed with lemon juice.

INGREDIENTS:

2 cups bulgar (12 oz)
1 lb ground lean lamb or beef
1 cup chopped onion
1 tsp butter
¼ cup pine nuts
½ tsp cinnamon
salt to taste

oil for deep-frying

Yields **24** dumplings

1. Cover bulgar with cold water and allow to soak for 15 minutes until grains have softened but are still a bit crunchy. Drain and pulse in food processor until bulgar starts to stick together and form a ball. Add more ice-cold water, a tablespoon at a time, if the bulgar doesn't stick together. Add half of the ground meat and half of the onions and pulse off and on until blended. Do not over-process. Bulgar should be nubby, not too smooth and hold together in a ball but not overly sticky. Add salt and pan-fry a little piece to taste so you can adjust the seasonings. Set aside in the refrigerator while you prepare the filling.

2. In a sauté pan over medium-high heat, add pine nuts. Toss until pine nuts are lightly toasted. Remove to mixing bowl. Return pan to heat and add butter, cinnamon and remaining onions. When onions begin to turn translucent, add remaining ground meat and cook until browned, stirring frequently and breaking meat into small crumbles. Season to taste with salt. Remove from heat and add to bowl of pine nuts. Mix well.

3. Form kibbeh by taking a golf-ball sized piece of dough in wet hands, pushing your finger into the middle of the ball and turning it in the palm of your other hand until a hollow egg-shape has formed with ¼" thick wall of dough. Into the pocket, or hollow of this egg shape, put a rounded teaspoon of meat filling. Gently push the dough closed around the top of the egg shape, smoothing holes closed with wet fingers, completely enclosing the filling. Set aside on a cookie sheet and repeat until all the dough and meat has been formed into filled dumplings. If you like, you can shape them into little tongues at this point by flattening them slightly and pressing with a chopstick or pencil down the middle of each one to make the centre furrow characteristic of tongues.

4. In a heavy pot or deep fryer, heat 3" of oil to 300°F or until a cube of white bread turns brown in 8 seconds. Gently slide 4 or 5 Kibbeh into the hot oil and fry on all sides til deep brown. Remove to draining rack and repeat until all Kibbeh are cooked. If you prefer not to deep-fry, Kibbeh Tongues can be brushed with melted butter and baked at 375° for 15-20 min. or until the shells are cooked and develop a golden brown crispy crust.

Easy Baggie Bungless Blood Sausage (104)

Jack and Hannibal talk in circles as they dine on Blood Sausage in episode 4, Season 1. Sausages made from the blood of a rabbit. "Should have hopped faster", says Jack, digging into Will's childhood as he digs into dinner. Hunger is stronger than sympathy.

For the shoot, I made vegetarian blood sausages out of pumpernickel and beets. Under the lights of the studio the real blood sausages lose their sinister ruby glow and just go crusty black. Besides which, I didn't relish the thought of making dozens of traditionally made blood sausages. It can turn into a horrible steaming mess – just re-read Zola's description in Belly of Paris and you will get the whole visceral idea!

If, like me, you do not relish the idea of squishing a bloody mash into a slippery gut, or having blood spray out all over the kitchen when your bung springs a leak, this recipe is for you! You can still have the traditional filling made from blood, but without the mess of sausage-making. Simply ladle the mixture into plastic zipper bags and poach it up! Voila, big fat sausages – just without the casings. These are like Morcilla, the soft, rice-filled Colombian-style blood sausage.

If you make a big batch, slice and freeze whatever you can't eat within 3 days then you can thaw and pan-fry a few slices whenever you have a hankering for these rich dark flavours.

Blood usually comes in half-litres, but it freezes well so you can pour off the quantity you need for this recipe and freeze the rest for future use.

INGREDIENTS:

½ onion, chopped
1 tsp butter
2 slices bacon, chopped
1 cup cooked rice
½ tsp salt
½ cup cooked peas (optional)
1 tsp rubbed oregano
½ cup panko breadcrumbs
1 cup fresh blood
1 egg
¼ cup heavy cream

2 small sandwich-sized zipper plastic food bags
4 large binder clips

Yields 2 "sausages"

1. Melt butter in a sauté pan over medium heat and add onions, cooking until translucent. Add bacon and stir until bacon is cooked but not crisp. Set aside.

2. In a second bowl, beat egg and stir in cream and blood. Add onion-bacon mixture, rice, peas, oregano and salt and breadcrumbs. Stir together until well combined. Put half into each baggie and zip partially closed. Push the contents to the bottom of the baggies and press the rest of the air out, zipping tightly closed.

3. Bring a large saucepan of water to boil over high heat. Lower heat til water simmers. Place the handle of a mixing spoon on the top of the saucepan, balancing on the sides and clip the top edge of a filled baggie to the spoon handle so the baggie is suspended upright in the water. Repeat with a second spoon and the other filled baggie. Allow the baggies to poach in very gently simmering water for 12-15 minutes or until mixture is firm. Cut into the centre of the filling to make sure the blood is cooked all the way through.

4. To serve, slice "sausages" into rounds ½-inch thick and brown in a sauté pan with a splash of oil for 2-3 minutes per side over medium heat, just until crispy and very dark brown. Don't turn the heat up too high as the slices burn easily.

CHIYOH'S ROAST PHEASANT (301)

In the spirit of a thousand cranes, Lady Murasaki's maid, Chiyoh, shot, plucked, roasted and wrapped an endless number of pheasants while attending her crazed prisoner at Lecter's castle. Tao Okamoto, the gifted Japanese supermodel who played Chiyoh was lovely and strong but didn't touch one bird. Unlike your loyal food stylist and the stalwart Chiyoh-double who toiled in Studio B's dark atmosphere of bird fat and flying feathers for weeks on end while the 2nd unit team captured the scenes of Chiyoh dispatching pheasants.

Many pheasants were sacrificed at the Altar of The Perfect Shot. At least now, I can tell you how to roast pheasant so they are moist and golden. Not because I did it – no, I was too busy on set plucking, chopping, tossing and tying. It was lovely Ettie, my first assistant who waited anxiously for the butcher's van and tended the oven fires day and night, basting the birds to golden goodness so we could have them in time for each day's early call.

INGREDIENTS:

1 pheasant (about 3 lb)
¼ cup butter, melted
salt and pepper to taste

Yields **2** servings

1. Tie the wings behind the pheasant's back and tie the legs together loosely with butcher's twine. Place on baking sheet or broiling pan. Brush liberally with butter and place in oven preheated to 350°F. Roast for 50 minutes, brushing with more butter every 12-15 minutes. To test for doneness, prick the inside of the thigh. Juice should run pale pink. If juices are red, return to oven for 10 more minutes at the most. Remove and allow to rest for 15 minutes before serving. Excellent with roast potatoes or wild rice.

QUAIL STUFFED WITH SWEET-BREADS AND HAZELNUTS

One of the most famous, now illegal, gourmet indulgences in French cuisine is roast ortolans. Favoured by gourmands since Roman times, these tiny wild songbirds are no bigger than your thumb. They are captured and caged in the dark so, thinking it's night-feeding time, they gorge on berries and grains until their bodies are so distended they can no longer stand. Plump with yellow fat, they are then drowned in Armagnac, plucked, nestled naked in a cocotte and seared in a hot oven to cook in their own fat. They are eaten whole, in one mouthful – tiny bones crunching as the hot fat and juices gush from Armagnac-filled lungs mixing with flesh and the faint taste of gut.

Will and Hannibal devour a pair of ortolans and we all shared their gastro-ecstasy in tantalizing close-ups. In this recipe, the sweetbreads provide the hint of offal flavor that I imagine makes ortolan so delicious. Armagnac, figs and hazelnuts add the flavour notes and crunch that ortolan connoisseurs speak of so rapturously.

INGREDIENTS:

12 oz sweetbreads
3 dried figs, cut in ¼" diced
¼ cup Armagnac, cognac or brandy
4 Tbsp butter
2 Tbsp chopped hazelnuts
4 slices bacon, chopped
½ cup diced shallots
3 Tbsp panko breadcrumbs
salt, pepper to taste
6 quails

2 main servings, or **6** appetizers.

1. Soak figs for at least 2 hours in Armagnac then drain. Set figs aside. Soak sweetbreads overnight covered in water, changing to fresh water several times. Drain and rinse well. In a medium-sized saucepan, cover sweetbreads with cold water and bring to boil over high heat. Turn heat to low and simmer for 10 minutes. Drain and rinse under cold water to stop cooking. Peel off and discard outer membrane and connective tissue, breaking the gland down into small ½" lobes. Set aside.

2. In a large sauté pan, melt 3 Tbsp butter over medium-low heat. Add shallots and cook slowly until gold and translucent. Turn up heat to medium and add hazelnuts. Cook stirring constantly until nuts have browned. Transfer to a bowl, set aside and return pan to heat. Add chopped bacon, sweetbreads, figs, breadcrumbs, salt and pepper to taste. Mix thoroughly and cook for a few minutes – just long enough to cook bacon and brown the breadcrumbs. Remove from heat and allow to cool.

3. Using paper towel, dry the quail inside and out. Sprinkle salt and pepper inside and out. Stuff the cavity of each quail with sweetbread mixture. Thread a toothpick through each cavity opening to keep stuffing from falling out. Tie legs of each bird together with butcher's string.

4. Preheat oven to 400°F. Prepare baking sheet by loosely crumpling a large sheet of foil over the entire surface. Place stuffed quail spaced evenly on the foil and press them down so the foil keeps the birds from tipping. Brush liberally with butter. Roast for 15 minutes or until lightly browned. Rest for 10 minutes, remove string and toothpicks and serve. If you wish, flambé them at the table: To flambé, put a tablespoon of Armagnac in a small ladle and hold it over a flame to heat. When warm, lower ladle and tip toward flame to ignite the fumes of the Armagnac. Pour flaming Armagnac over the quails. Flame will go out once alcohol is exhausted.

CLAY-BAKED CHICKEN (202)

I've noticed it's a little difficult to get men's thighs at the butcher shops, so instead of a recipe for Gideon's thigh from Season 2's *Futamono*, I'm offering one that will be slightly more useful: clay-baked whole chicken. After all, they have double the thigh meat and are not nearly as much trouble to push into an oven.

You can purchase clay from any arts and hobby shop that carries pottery supplies. This packaged clay has all been sterilized and is food-safe.

INGREDIENTS:

one 3½ lb chicken
10 strips bacon
¼ tsp paprika
¼ tsp salt
2 cloves garlic, crushed
1 lemon, cut in half
1 sprig rosemary

1 dried lotus leaf, softened in water*
10 lb potter's clay
baking parchment

Dried lotus leaves can be bought in Asian grocery stores. Rinse and soak in warm water to soften before using. Substitute: a large piece of baking parchment or aluminium foil.

Yields **3** main course servings

1. With a rolling pin, roll one-third of the potter's clay ¼" thick on a sheet of baking parchment and trim the clay into an oval about 10" x 7". Place the clay on a large baking sheet. Roll out remaining clay on another sheet of baking parchment to ¼" thickness and set aside.

2. Using a mortar and pestle, or a small bowl and the back of a spoon, grind together the salt and garlic. Mix in the paprika. Rub the chicken all over with this spice mix. Put the lemon halves and the rosemary inside the chicken cavity and tie the legs together.

3. Lay 5 strips of bacon side by side on the diagonal to cover the chicken. Lay the remaining strips of bacon on the opposite diagonal and weave the strips together covering the entire top of chicken. Transfer chicken to the middle of the soaked lotus leaf or parchment paper and wrap snugly to cover chicken. Place this package onto the middle of the small oval of clay. Lift the larger sheet of clay over the chicken package and press down firmly so the upper sheet of clay reaches the bottom layer of clay and covers the entire chicken. Pinch the two sheets of clay together to create an airtight seal. Decorate with flowers and leaves made from the clay trimmings.

4. In an oven pre-heated to 325°F, roast the clay-enclosed chicken for 1 hour then turn the heat up to 400° and roast for another 20 minutes. Remove from oven and allow to rest for 15 minutes. Transfer to a cutting board or large tray and present at the table. Crack open the clay, remove all the clay shards, peel back lotus leaf or parchment, then carve and serve the chicken.

THE FIFTH QUARTER IN CARCIOFI CORATELLA

T his traditional Roman dish uses coratella, or the "fifth quarter" of a freshly slaughtered lamb. Hannibal explains to his eager dinner guests that in ancient times, the first quarter – or best cuts would go to nobility, the second quarter to the clergy, third to the bourgeoisie and the fourth quarter would go to the military. The slaughterhouse workers were often paid with the remaining offal was dubbed the Quint Quarto or fifth quarter.

Hannibal's recipe calls for skewers of sautéed lung and liver and the hearts of the gorgeous purple artichokes one finds in Florence. Here's a quick and delicious version using roasted chicken instead of offal and canned artichoke hearts instead of whole purple artichokes. Serve with a leafy salad.

CARCIOFI CHICKEN (303)

INGREDIENTS:

1½ cups canned artichoke hearts,
   drained and quartered
3 cups boneless roasted chicken meat,
   cut in 1" cubes

For the sauce:
5 Tbsp butter
5 Tbsp flour
2½ cups strong chicken stock
2 chicken broth concentrate cubes
½ cup white wine
3 Tbsp lemon juice
salt and pepper to taste

For topping:
4 Tbsp melted butter
3-6 cloves garlic, crushed
1½ cups breadcrumbs, preferably
   Japanese-style panko

Yields **4** main course servings

1. In a large heavy-bottomed saucepan, melt butter over medium-high heat and add flour. Stir over medium-high heat until golden brown. Remove from heat and add chicken stock, chicken cubes, white wine, and lemon juice, stirring constantly with whisk to smooth out lumps. When smooth, return to heat and boil gently until thickened, whisking occasionally. If any lumps persist, press sauce through a sieve.

2. Add artichokes and chicken and stir gently until sauce coats all evenly. Turn into a 9" x 9" ovenproof dish and set aside.

3. In a medium-sized bowl, stir melted butter and garlic together. Add breadcrumbs and toss until well blended. Spread evenly over chicken mixture. Bake at 350°F for 20 minutes or until filling is bubbling and topping is golden brown.

PANTHE KOW SWEY (110)

This fragrant curried chicken noodle stew is the national dish of Burma and I think you'll find it easier to make and more fun to eat than the Aatu Kudal Kulambu that Hannibal makes for Chilton from sheep's intestines in Episode 10 of Season 1. For the scene, I made a curry with a wild assortment of pasta shapes that looked so much like cooked entrails no one wanted to taste it. Raul asked for a "spit bucket" (a vessel actors sometimes request so they can spit out the bites of food they "eat" during a food scene). Quitter.

INGREDIENTS:

½ chicken, boned and cut in pieces
   about 1" x ½" x ½"
2 Tbsp crushed garlic
1 Tbsp grated ginger
1 large onion, finely chopped
¼ tsp chili powder
2 tsp turmeric
¼ tsp salt
¼ cup oil
1 cup coconut milk
¾ cup chicken cooking liquid or water
2 cups warm, cooked, drained thick rice
   noodles or egg noodles

Accompaniments:
1 small bowl chopped tomatoes
1 small bowl chopped green onion
1 small bowl chopped coriander leaves
1 small bowl boiled egg, diced
1 small bowl lime wedges
1 small bowl pan-fried dried whole
   chillies
1 small bowl crisp-fried onion bits
1 small bowl crisp-fried garlic bits

Yields 4 servings

1. In a bowl, mix together chicken, garlic, ginger, onion, chili, turmeric, salt and oil. Heat a large heavy pot over high heat. Add chicken mixture and fry, stirring lightly (do not brown). Remove from heat and add enough water to cover meat. Bake uncovered in pre-heated oven at 350°F for 30 min. Remove chicken from cooking liquid, strain cooking liquid and reserve ¾ cup, adding water if necessary.

2. Combine chicken, reserved cooking liquid and coconut milk in a large saucepan and simmer over low heat for 15 minutes. When ready to serve, place a portion of noodles in four large soup bowls, add chicken pieces, spoon liquid over that and serve. Place the small bowls of accompaniments in the centre of the table, encouraging guests to generously sprinkle accompaniments on top of their Kow Swey as they eat it. To make banana leaf bowls as Hannibal did for rice bowls or for the individual accompaniments, see (p226).

Ravenstag Stew

U se a tougher cut like shoulder for the venison in this stew. The long, slow cooking will make it fork-tender. This recipe will serve six. You could serve half of it as stew with buttery mashed potatoes and warm crusty bread and then freeze the rest for Deerly Beloved Meat Pies (p115) to enjoy another day. Stagger the stag so to speak.

Hannibal is always slipping something into the food of his unsuspecting guests. Gin, not people, is my secret ingredient in this stew but don't keep it a secret from your guests…regale them, Hannibal-style, with the saucy information that wild venison eat juniper berries and this improves their flavour. Gin is made with juniper berries and also carries their distinctive taste. Hence, the addition of gin to the stew accents this woodsy richness. If you can't find juniper berries, double the gin. If you don't have gin, double the berries. If you have neither, throw in a handful of blueberries and carry on cooking…the stew will still be delicious.

Ingredients:

For venison:
1 tsp salt
⅓ cup flour
2 lb stewing venison cut into 1" cubes
3 Tbsp olive oil

For stew:
1 cup red wine
1½ cups water
1 tsp beef stock concentrate
1 Tbsp gin
1 Tbsp dried juniper berries
1 tsp dried Italian oregano leaves
1 medium onion, rough chopped in 1" pieces
2 medium carrots, rough chopped in 1" pieces
1 medium parsnip, rough chopped in 1" pieces
⅓ cup dried prunes, pitted chopped

salt and pepper, to taste

Yields **6** servings

1. In a large bowl, combine flour and salt. Add venison cubes and toss to coat well.

2. In a large heavy pot with lid, heat half of the olive oil over high heat, add half of the venison and turn to brown all sides. Remove to bowl. Repeat with remaining venison. Add water to pot and deglaze by scraping any bits off the bottom of the pot. Return browned venison to the pot and bring to a boil, stirring as sauce thickens. Add remaining ingredients.

3. Turn heat to very low and simmer gently for 2-3 hours. Do not allow the stew to boil – bubbles should just gently break the surface of the liquid. Stir occasionally to scrape up anything that is sticking to the bottom of the pot. Sauce should thicken as flour cooks and vegetables melt, but add water if too much liquid evaporates. Add salt and pepper if desired.

DEERLY BELOVED MEAT PIES

You can bake these in any oven-proof containers like cocottes, ramekins, oven-proof soup bowls or little individual-sized pie pans, as long as they will hold the filling leaving enough room at the top for the filling to boil and bubble as the pastry cooks. Filling should be chilled when making the pies so the pastry doesn't start melting before it goes into the oven.

INGREDIENTS:

2 cups cold Ravenstag Stew (about half
  of the opposite recipe)
1 batch Lemon Olive Oil pastry (p116)

Yields **2** individual portion pies

1. Roll each round of chilled pastry to an 8-in diameter circle and line two 4-inch pie pans or oven-proof bowls with a round of pastry each.

2. Spoon half of the stew into each of the lined pans, mounding it up in the middle. Moisten edge of pastry lining with water and cover each with a round of pastry. Press dough of bottom and top rounds together and crimp all the way around the rim to enclose filling. Cut slashes in the top pastry to allow steam to escape during baking.

3. Bake pies in an oven preheated to 400°F for 10 minutes then reduce to 350°F and bake for another 15 to 20 minutes or until pastry is golden brown and filling is heated through.

STAG PARTY

Episode 103 has no food in it. This was a terrible shock to me to be sidelined so early in the series. I had read the script over and over in disbelief – thinking I had somehow skimmed over the food scene. But no. Just pages and pages of stags stalking the hallways, hiding in the bushes and bolting down the ravine. A cook cannot see frame after frame of this magnificent animal without thinking of venison and its many delights. So in honour of Ravenstag, Wendigo, the Shrike Stag and Spooky Baby Stagenstein, here are a few of my favorite venison dishes.

LEMON AND OLIVE OIL PASTRY

This is a pâte brisée style of pastry that is not as fragile as flaky pastry, so it's excellent for containing the juices of savoury pies like Deerly Beloved and Beverly Steak and Kidney Pie (p89). If you want your pies to have a shiny glaze, use the left-over egg white mixed with a ¼ cup of milk to make an egg wash to brush over the pastry. But watch closely as the glaze can burn quickly! One batch is enough to make one double-crust pie or two individual meat pies.

INGREDIENTS:

2 cups flour

¼ tsp salt

½ cup cold unsalted butter, roughly cut in ½" cubes

2 Tbsp olive oil

1 egg yolk

¼ cup ice-cold water or chilled white wine

¼ tsp grated lemon rind

Yields pastry for **1** large double crust or **2** individual pies

Yields **2** servings

1. In a small bowl, combine oil, yolk, water and lemon juice. Beat together until well combined. Set aside in refrigerator.

2. In a cold large mixing bowl, combine salt and flour then add butter cubes. Cut butter into flour using pastry cutter or two knives until mixture resembles crumbled oatmeal in texture. Add yolk mixture and toss together lightly with a fork until the dough starts to clump together as you stir. Once the flour and liquids have gathered together in a ball, turn dough out of bowl onto floured board and knead very lightly several times just until it is smooth. Dough will be soft but should not stick to your fingers. Shape into two balls, flatten balls slightly and cover with plastic wrap. Refrigerate for at least 1 hour. You can make this dough up to 3 days ahead if you keep it refrigerated, or several months ahead if you keep it in the freezer.

Beef Rib Eye Steak
with Snail Sauce (206)

Z eller and Price come for Hannibal just when he is taking a little roast beef out of the oven. They are bringing him in for cannibal questioning, so for the scene, I wanted the roast to be obviously not human but still very Hannibal. I chose the largest roast one might come by…a custom-cut 7-bone prime rib but with the ribs left long and Frenched. It was massive! So huge, in fact it wouldn't fit in the oven so, sadly I had to cut it down.

But size is not enough. How could I give it Hannibal's signature? Dress it in plaid, of course! I scored it in crosshatch and laced the cuts with sprigs of herbs so it resembled a meaty MacGregor tartan. Then threw on a few snails for good measure. There are few things as unexpectedly delicious as snail sauce on beef.

In case your oven isn't as big as Hannibal's, I've converted the recipe from rib roast to rib steaks – just as splendid.

INGREDIENTS:

2 rib-eye beef steaks, thick cut
1 Tbsp oil

2 peeled drumstick shallots, one cut in
    half lengthwise, one minced
2 Tbsp butter
1 clove garlic
½ cup red wine
½ cup beef or veal stock

1 dozen Burgundian snails
1 dozen button mushrooms
2 strips of thick-cut pancetta bacon,
    diced
1 Tbsp parsley
1 sprig rosemary
salt and pepper to taste

2 cups hot buttery mashed potatoes

Yields 2 main course servings

1. Start the snail sauce by heating half of the butter in a large, heavy-bottomed skillet over medium heat. Add bacon, minced shallot and garlic. Cook until shallots and bacon begin to turn translucent. Add mushrooms and cook until shallots are translucent and mushrooms are releasing juice. Deglaze skillet by adding wine and stock, scraping up any bits from the pan. Boil until wine has reduced to half volume. Remove to a bowl and set aside.

2. Wipe skillet clean, return to high heat and add oil. When pan is hot, place steaks in skillet but do not crowd. Add halved shallot, cut side down. Fry steaks and shallots on both sides. Remove shallots when translucent and cut edges have browned, then break shallot layers apart into cup-shaped shells. Continue frying steaks for total of 4 minutes on each side. Remove to platter and keep in warming oven until the sauce is ready or the FBI agents leave.

3. Transfer sauce mixture back into skillet and bring to boil over medium heat, scraping up bits to deglaze pan. Add snails, parsley, rosemary and any juice from the platter that has drained from the steaks and bring to boil. When the sauce comes to a boil, remove from heat, remove rosemary, and whisk in remaining butter. Plate by placing a dollop of mashed potatoes in the middle of each plate, a steak on top of that and shallot halves on top of steak, cup sides up. Pour snail sauce over steaks, tipping a snail into each shallot cup and serve.

Venison Medallions with Seared Foie Gras (305)

When you buy fresh foie gras, it is usually vacuum-packed in whole lobes and is rarely sold in smaller packages. You only need a quarter of a lobe for this recipe but you can freeze what you don't use as it freezes very well and it's always good to have a bit of foie in the freezer for impromptu celebrations.

Venison is best eaten rare or medium-rare. It's very lean and will become quite dry if overcooked. This is delicious served with steamed potatoes and needs no sauce but if you wish, you can accompany the venison with a store-bought demi-glace sauce or Duxelles (p101) or Sage Plum Berry Sauce (p32).

Verger's spies must have drooled green as they monitored Hannibal's invidious Florentine life. He relished this serving of venison using antique Christofle silverware to lift the blood-rare bites from his gold-trimmed Tiffany china to his curling lips.

INGREDIENTS:

four 1½" thick venison tenderloin
   medallions
¼ lobe of fresh foie gras
flour for dredging
4 tsp oil
salt, pepper to taste

Yields **2** servings

1. Prepare foie gras for searing: cut the lobe into slices about ½" thick. They should be about 2"x1" in size. Dredge the slices in flour and set aside in the refrigerator.

2. Heat 1 Tbsp of oil in a sauté pan or heavy skillet over medium-high heat. Add medallions to pan and cook on each side for 3-4 minutes until rare or medium-rare. Season with salt to taste. Remove from pan and place on heat-proof tray in a warm oven. Prepare dinner plates now because you will want to serve them as soon as the foie is cooked.

3. Wipe sauté pan clean and return to heat. Add just a bit of oil. Not much is needed as foie will release sufficient oil as it cooks. Add foie to pan and cook just until it begins to brown. Turn over and cook on other side until it browns. Don't cook too long or the foie gras will melt away. The slices should be very pink inside. Season with salt and pepper to taste. Remove immediately. Place venison on serving plates and one piece of seared foie gras on each medallion and serve.

TENDERLOIN OF BEEF IN A TENT FOR TWO (109)

Fabulous Freddie Lounds, incendiary newshound, joins Abigail and Will at Hannibal's table. He's serving Roast Tenderloin, not realizing that Freddie is a vegetarian. He makes a dazzling but eerie salad of pods and roots that would send any diner into a trypophobic panic. But not Freddie. She's made of sterner stuff. She navigates her dinner plate, made of bone china, and eats her salad garnished with bird skulls, asparagus as white as finger bones and Munch-worthy slices of scream-faced lotus root. For Abigail, Will and Hannibal, the slices of tenderloin were roasted rare and I sent them out to set with a little ooze of raspberry purée on top to emphasize the bloodiness.

Here's a recipe for rare roasted tenderloin that is easy to make yet impressive in its presentation. When the silvery tent is opened at the table, the room is suffused in the heady aroma of roast and rosemary.

INGREDIENTS:

1 piece tenderloin tip (about 1½ lb)
1 Tbsp oil
2 marrow bones, 4-inch long and
    canoe-cut in half
salt, pepper to taste
2 branches fresh rosemary

l large piece of aluminum cooking foil

Yields **2-3** servings,
or **4** if one is a vegetarian

1. In a hot skillet over high heat, heat 1Tbsp oil, brown cut side of marrow bones, about 2 minutes then turn and cook cut side up for 2 minutes. Remove from skillet and place bones, marrow side up, in centre of 16" x 24" piece of heavy foil that has been placed on a cookie sheet.

2. Fold narrow end of tenderloin under and tie with butchers twine to equalize circumference along the length of the roast. Add tenderloin to hot skillet and sear on all sides (about 4 minutes). Remove from skillet and place tenderloin on top of bones, sprinkle with salt and pepper to taste, top with herbs and pull foil up around it, enclosing all in a very loose tent. Crimp foil closed, leaving lots of room all around the roast.

3. Roast in 425° oven for 15 minutes or until rare. Open the foil packet at the table and enjoy the aroma. Serve with frites or pan-roasted potatoes.

SERVED PLATED:

SALAD of GREENS + ROOT CHIPS with SLICES of RARE ROAST TENDERLOIN

BIRDSKULL
POMEGRANATE SEED SPATTER

JUS

SPINACH-STUFFED VEAL WITH CUMBERLAND SAUCE (102)

Why veal? Because, according to William Seabrook, that's exactly what human flesh tastes like. Back in the 1930s, he was a reporter for The New York Times and, researching cannibalism for a book, asked a med-student friend at the Sorbonne to procure for him a piece of healthy human flesh. He cooked it up and promptly declared it to be stringy but delicious – and tasting exactly like a good piece of veal. So instead of the pork that Hannibal claims he is serving to Jack, we are substituting veal. Or, if you like, substitute pork loin – think "Long Pig."

When I'm food styling, I never use any food that might stick to the front tooth of an actor and ruin a take. Not having the same concerns, you will want to stuff as much buttery spinach into the strip loin as possible because it's delicious!

INGREDIENTS:

For stuffing:
three 6-oz bags of spinach, washed, stems removed
½ cup butter
2 cups mushrooms, in ¼" slices
1 clove crushed garlic
1 tomato, chopped
1 cup panko breadcrumbs
salt, pepper to taste

For roast:
1 veal strip loin, about 2 lb
4-6 slices bacon
Salt, pepper

Yields **4** servings

1. Place a half bag of washed spinach leaves in a plastic zipper bag. Zip partially closed, leaving at least 1" open for steam to escape. Microwave for 90 seconds. Remove to a strainer to drain. Using the back of a spoon, press out as much liquid as possible. Repeat with remaining spinach. Coarsely chop the spinach and put in medium-sized mixing bowl. Add tomato to bowl, mix together and set aside.

2. In a sauté pan over high heat, add 2 Tbsp of the butter, a third of the garlic and a third of the mushrooms. Cook until moisture is released from mushrooms and evaporated off. Season to taste with salt and pepper and add to bowl of spinach. Repeat with remaining mushrooms.

3. Over medium high heat, melt the remaining butter in a sauté pan and add breadcrumbs. Cook, stirring constantly, until lightly browned. Add to bowl of spinach and mix together until all ingredients are thoroughly blended. Add salt and pepper to taste.

4. Preheat oven to 375°F.

5. With a sharp slicing or boning knife, slice a pocket in the veal to within ½" of the sides. See diagram (opposite). Season inside of this pocket liberally with salt and pepper and stuff firmly with spinach/mushroom mixture. Transfer to a roasting pan and place slices of bacon on top.

6. Roast for 40 minutes or until veal is medium-rare. Rest for 15 min before slicing. Serve with Cumberland Sauce, right.

Cumberland Sauce

Recommended by Chef José Andrés for our first episode, this was to become my favourite sauce for *Hannibal*. It is viscid, velvety and crimson. Slowly dripping down a roast leg or swirled on his stark white china, Cumberland Sauce has all the evocative qualities of thickening blood but none of the unhappy circumstances.

To make the raspberry purée, thaw frozen raspberries and press through a sieve with the back of a large spoon. This will remove seeds and result in a velvety smooth purée. A 12-oz bag of frozen berries will yield about 1½ cups. This purée is great just as it is, as a topping for ice cream or chocolate cake or to dress a fruit salad. Or punch it up a notch and make it into this modified Cumberland Sauce to serve with pork and lamb.

INGREDIENTS:

1 cup raspberry purée
1 Tbsp frozen orange juice concentrate
½ cup port
1 Tbsp red currant jelly
pinch cayenne (optional)

Yields **1½** cups

1. Combine all ingredients in a small saucepan and bring to boil over medium heat. Boil for a few minutes then remove from heat. Serve warm.

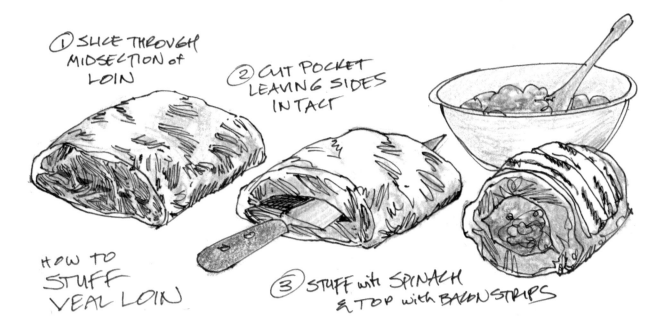

① SLICE THROUGH MIDSECTION of LOIN

② CUT POCKET LEAVING SIDES INTACT

HOW TO STUFF VEAL LOIN

③ STUFF with SPINACH & TOP with BACON STRIPS

RACK OF SACRIFICIAL LAMB (213)

Roast whole baby lamb is indescribably delicious and delicate but needs a very large oven and a big group of people to eat it. Plus it can be tricky getting a baby lamb at the corner store – it is a seasonal item, so here is an alternative recipe for regular rack of lamb – still deliciously yummy but easy to get.

If you want to make them into "Praying Hands Lamb" as Hannibal made for Will, ask your butcher to leave the bones long and French the racks. Before roasting, place the racks upright on the roasting pan, bones curved toward each other. Using poultry shears, clip the first bone of each rack so it is shorter, like a thumb. Using butcher's twine, tie the next four pairs of bones together to look like the fingers praying hands. Splay the remaining ribs out. Use crumpled foil to keep everything in place as the lamb cooks. I've given two flavours to choose from: a French herb rub or an Asian marinade.

INGREDIENTS:

2 racks of lamb (5 – 8 bones each)

Style One: Herb Rub:
¼ cup olive oil
3 to 4 cloves of garlic, crushed
3 sprigs rosemary, stems removed
to taste crushed pepper, sea salt

Style Two: Spicy peanut marinade
1 4-oz bar coconut cream
2 Tbsp water
6 Tbsp peanut butter
1 Tbsp chili sauce
2 Tbsp soy sauce
3 Tbsp Satay sauce, sweet soy or Hoi Sin sauce
2 cloves garlic crushed

Yields **2-4** main course servings

1. In a small bowl, combine all ingredients and rub into lamb.

2. Roast in preheated oven at 425° for 20 to 25 minutes or until medium rare. Rest for 10 minutes and slice and serve.

Or if you want to try Malaysian barbecue and can start a day or two ahead:

1. In a small saucepan, melt coconut cream in water over medium heat, cool and stir in peanut butter, chili sauce, satay sauce and garlic. Spoon over lamb and marinate, refrigerated, overnight or up to 2 days. Reserve excess marinade for basting during cooking.

2. Fire up the BBQ (or preheat the broiler) and barbecue 12-15 minutes or until medium rare or broil 4-5 minutes per side. Brush with reserved marinade. Allow to rest for 10 minutes and slice and serve.

ROAST SUCKLING PIG (210)

Hannibal served sucking pig to Alana and Will just before their ménage à trois in *Naka-Choko*. I made so many trips to the studio with suckling pigs strapped in my car that I could have gotten a permanent permit for the multi-occupancy lanes. It amazes me now to realize that I only used suckling pig for one dinner scene and one for Will's hallucidinner. We reshot the scene for *Naka-Choko* more than a few times and I got really good at piglet-wrangling.

This looks hard but is really easy. The hardest part is getting a pan to fit the pig to fit your oven. You could try putting two shallow sided pans side by side and covering them as one with several layers of tinfoil. The pig you can get by calling an Italian butcher or a local farm that raises organic pigs.

INGREDIENTS:

Rub:
1 Tbsp dried rosemary leaves
1 Tbsp dried oregano leaves
1 tsp rubbed dried sage leaves
2 Tbsp coarse sea salt

olive oil

1 suckling pig, about 15-20 lb (or to fit your oven)

2 oranges halved
1 lemon, halved
4 shallots, halved

Yields **6-10** main course servings

1. Preheat oven to 300°F and line the baking pan with parchment or foil.

2. In a small bowl or large mortar, crush together rosemary, oregano, sage and salt.

3. With a large heavy knife such as a cleaver, make a vertical slash through the skin and meat of the pig's neck along the vertebrae between the shoulder blades (about 4 inches long) This is to keep the skin from cracking when it browns and crisps. If necessary, sever the leg joints so you can tuck the legs in closer to the body. Turn pig over and sprinkle herb-salt mixture in the chest cavity and rub onto the entire interior surface.

4. Place the pig on its side on the baking pan and stuff the chest cavity with the orange, lemon and shallots, tie its legs together if necessary, then roll it upright so it is sitting on its belly. Pig should be room temperature at this point to ensure even cooking. Wrap its ears and tail with foil to keep them from burning.

5. Place in oven and roast for 12 minutes per pound, or until thermometer reads 150°F. Brushing with oil occasionally. Skin should be very soft and meat just undercooked at this point. Turn the oven up to 450°F. Roast for another 45 min to 1 hr or until skin is golden brown and crisp.

6. Remove from oven and allow to rest for an hour before serving. This will give you plenty of time to mound fruit, steamed rice or Cauliflower Peas Pilaf (p152) around it attractively.

Bedelia's Kalua Roasted Loin (313)

A true kalua roast is wrapped in banana leaves, placed in a deep pit on top of smoldering embers of mesquite, piled with hot rocks and buried. It's left overnight to slow-cook in the sandy earth until the meat is fork-tender then dug up and eaten the next day. It's a perfect way to cook the lean muscle of a romantic rival.

But even if you could get one, you don't really want to eat a people-leg, do you? And it's hard to dig a 4-foot pit on the deck of your condo. So here is a recipe for Hawaiian Long Pig Loin dressed to kill for an off-beach luau for eight.

Ask your butcher to cut an extra-long pork loin about 14" long. It will be about 2½ pounds. By getting this special cut, the roast will have dimensions closer to Bedelia's thigh, plus you get to legitimately call it "long pig" on your menu. I stitched and glued (with transglutaminase – go ahead, Google "meat glue") four of these long loins onto a beef bone and a lamb shank for each leg I made for Gideon. For Bedelia's much more delicate leg, hip to ankle, I used three long loins.

INGREDIENTS:

1 boneless pork loin, extra long
1 large parsnip, optional
6-8 cloves garlic, peeled, cut in half
¼ cup honey
½ cup Dijon mustard
½ tsp dried rosemary, crushed

12 aspidistra or ti leaves (from florist), washed, stems removed
Flowers and fruit for garnish

Yields main course serving for 8-10

1. Shape the loin into a thigh: Place the loin on your working surface, fatty side down, short end toward you. Cut a long slash in the meat from top to bottom. Then, with your knife on a 30° angle and at the top edge of the loin (furthest away from you), trim out a cone of muscle 1" at the top graduating to 3"x 1" at the bottom (closest to you) from the muscle of the loin. Flip this cone over and place back with thick end at the top of the loin and thin end at the bottom.

2. Using a paring knife, poke deep cuts in the pork loin all over by plunging the tip of the knife straight into the meat to a depth of an inch or two. Into each cut, push a garlic clove.

3. Roll up loin from left to right with the fat on the outside and tie at 4" intervals with butcher's twine. If you think this makes your thigh look big, adjust the position of the cut cone until you like the proportions. Add more twine ties at 1" intervals to secure the shapeliness of your roast, except for the last section of the narrow end – this will be the knee. Place roast on a baking sheet with sides. If desired, push a half parsnip into the roll at either end to represent the bone.

4. In a small bowl, mix together honey, mustard and rosemary. Brush all over the roast. Place roast in an oven preheated to 350°F. Roast uncovered for 20 min per pound, or until meat thermometer reads 150°F basting frequently with mustard mixture and pan juices. Once taken out of the oven, it will continue to cook and the internal temperature will go up to the recommended temperature of 160° as it rests. Allow roast to rest for at least 30 minutes before slicing.

5. Prepare serving platter: secure leaves together in pairs by overlapping stem ends of two opposingly positioned leaves and skewering them together. Repeat with 4 or 5 more pairs – enough to span the length of the cooked roast. Lay the pairs on the serving tray side by side along the length of the tray. When the roast is fully cooked, remove from oven and place on top of leaves, covering the midline where the pairs are skewered together. One pair at a time, bring the leaf tips up and around the girth of the roast, pinch-pleat and secure together at the top of the roast with decorative picks. Repeat with leaf pairs down the full length of the roast until the whole roast is bound in leaves. Place fruits, flowers and extra leaves around the roast to decorate and serve. The leaves are for decorative purposes only, so when serving the roast, undo and push the leaves aside as you slice the roast.

Osso Buco (202)

There was tension on the set when we shot this scene – we only had one prosthetic leg to work with and Mads had never worked a butcher's band saw before. He had to get it in one take. Cutting the first slice was nerve-wracking because the latex of the fake leg stuck on the blade and jumped about madly. Tiny flecks of hot plastic flew in the air. We rubbed lubricant on the saw, Mads stepped in and the director yelled "Action!" The crew held their breath as Mads smoothly sawed the entire leg into lovely osso buco slices in one continuous shot. As the blade made its last slice, Mads threw the sawed-off foot over his head with a flourish. It landed in the sink, the director yelled "Cut!" and the crew erupted in applause and laughter.

Hannibal makes this dish with his secret ingredient, the muralist's lower leg. You can make a delicious, less diabolical version with veal – a calf of a more acceptable sort.

INGREDIENTS:

6 slices of bone-in veal shank, 2-2½" thick
½ cup flour
salt, pepper to taste
2 Tbsp olive oil

1 cup chopped onions
1 cup carrots in ¼" dice
1 cup celery in ¼" dice
½ cup parsnips in ¼" dice
2 Tbsp butter

1 cup beef stock (or chicken stock for lighter flavour)
1 cup red wine (or white wine for lighter flavour)
1½ cups fresh or canned chopped plum tomatoes

1 tsp dried oregano
1 sprig fresh rosemary
1 bay leaf

Yields **4** servings

1. Dredge veal pieces with flour and sprinkle with salt and pepper.

2. In a large Dutch oven or heavy lidded casserole, heat olive oil over medium-high heat then add veal pieces, sautéing on all sides til brown. Remove veal pieces to a bowl and set aside.

3. Add onions, carrots, celery and butter to Dutch oven and sauté, stirring over medium heat until lightly browned. Deglaze the Dutch oven by adding stock and scraping up all the browned bits from the bottom of the pan, then add wine, tomatoes, oregano, rosemary and bay leaf. Return veal shanks to the Dutch oven, cover and bake at 350°F for 1 hour then reduce to 275°F and bake for another 3-4 hours or until very tender. Check occasionally and add water if necessary to keep the shanks semi-submerged. Remove to serving dish, garnish with chopped parsley and lemon zest and serve with Saffron Risotto (p175) or noodles.

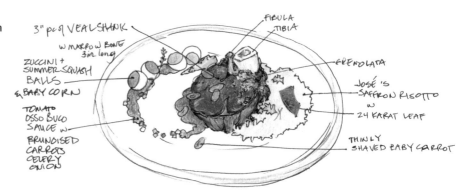

3" pc of VEAL SHANK
w MARROW BONE 3 in long
ZUCCINI + SUMMER SQUASH BALLS & BABY CORN
TOMATO OSSO BUCO SAUCE w BRUNOISED CARROTS CELERY ONION
FIBULA TIBIA
GREMOLATA
JOSÉ'S SAFFRON RISOTTO w 24 KARAT LEAF
THINLY SHAVED BABY CARROT

Deuxième Partie

HAVING FRIENDS
FOR DINNER

MAINS - FISH

DECONSTRUCTED SUSHI BOWL (201)

In the opening scenes of Season 2, Hannibal is preparing an elegant Japanese dinner for Jack. Kaiseki is the most elevated of Japanese cuisine. Our showrunner, Bryan Fuller, gave the names of its courses to the episodes of Season 3.

Kaiseki is an exquisitely complex dinner of many small courses made in studied harmony with the season. There are very strict traditions upheld in its presentation, so I called in Hashimoto, famed Kaiseki master, to attend the shoot to observe and advise me. Luckily for me, he was mortified by the lethal way I swung the knives around and completely took over the preparation of the food.

It was wonderful watching his knives fly masterfully and gracefully while I munched on Fritos from safety of the craft table.

Sashimi is an important component of Kaiseki and Hannibal presents his "flounder" on a deep-fried fishbone. Bryan wanted to be sure that a man's flesh could be disguised as fish. I showed him some research that described how the chicken industry once used peroxide to lighten the unpopular dark meat to appear white. People-meat would never look like flounder but it could be bleached to look like tuna, which has a meaty texture.

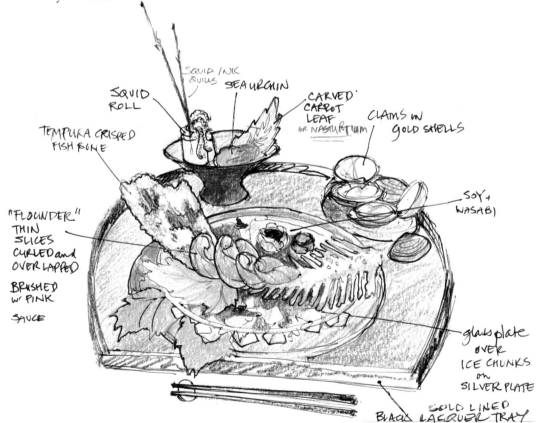

SQUID INK QUILLS

SEA URCHIN

SQUID ROLL

CARVED CARROT LEAF OR NASTURTIUM

CLAMS IN GOLD SHELLS

TEMPURA CRISPED FISH BONE

SOY + WASABI

"FLOUNDER" THIN SLICES CURLED and OVER LAPPED

BRUSHED w/ PINK

SAUCE

glass plate OVER ICE CHUNKS on SILVER PLATE

GOLD LINED BLACK LACQUER TRAY

Before every food scene, I clear the ingredients with the actors to check for preferences and dietary restrictions. Both Mads and Laurence immediately declared their love for Hamachi when I suggested yellowtail tuna. So I ordered 20 lb of it going with the premise that Hannibal never meant that the 'flounder' was a fish and he could easily have bleached the unfortunate fellow's flesh to resemble a meaty fish like tuna.

Here is sashimi presented on a bowl of vegetable-studded rice – a sort of deconstructed sushi that is easy to make and fun to eat. If you don't like raw fish, substitute poached shrimp, Japanese barbecued eel or fried tofu strips marinated in sweet soy.

INGREDIENTS:

For rice:

2 cups short grain Japanese rice (sushi rice)

3¾ cups water

4 tsp rice wine vinegar (mirin)

3 tsp sugar

½ tsp salt

For sushi:

¼ cup finely shredded carrot

¼ cup green peas

¼ cup finely shredded red bell pepper

8 oz sushi-grade salmon or tuna sliced in pieces 1" x 2" x ½"

½ tsp wasabi thinned with water to pouring consistency

1 sheet of nori (sushi seaweed) scissored into small slivers

1 Tbsp chopped green onion

2 Tbsp Spicy Mayo (below)

1. Cook rice with water in a rice cooker, following instructions, or on stovetop: in a heavy pot on high, allow rice and water to boil until water level is just below surface of the rice. Stir well, reduce heat to very low, secure lid tightly on top and allow to simmer for 20 minutes or until rice is soft. Remove from heat.

2. Prepare sushi rice seasoning by combining mirin, sugar and salt in a small pan over low heat until sugar melts. Pour over cooked rice and toss to combine. Add carrots, peas and peppers.

SPICY MAYO

An indispensible topping for spicy sushi and California rolls, this easy-to-make mayo is also great on French fries and as a salad or sandwich dressing. You can make your own mayonnaise for this or use a store-bought mayo. Kewpie is Japanese mayonnaise and is extra sweet.

Ingredients:

1 Tbsp chili sauce such as sriracha

¼ cup mayonnaise

1 tsp lime juice

1. In a small bowl, mix chili sauce, mayonnaise and lime juice. Refrigerate until ready to use.

CRAB PILAF (108)

"I wouldn't poison you, Tobias. I wouldn't do that to the food," Hannibal tells his paranoid dinner guest. So true – one must respect one's ingredients. As for guests, they are just another card filed under "rude" in his Rolodex.

To make the crab pilaf that Hannibal served, use the same ingredients as Paella on the Rocks (p138) but instead of clams, mussels and chicken, use two crabs. Frozen crabmeat is inferior so, sadly you must start with live Dungeness crab. They are very feisty and can be quite challenging to kill, so you might want to ask the fish seller to pull off the upper shell, remove the gills, the apron flap from the back and the small mandibles from the front. Get him to chop the body in 4-6 pieces to separate the legs, but make sure he leaves the dark buttery tomalley in the top shell.

With crabs thus dispatched, put the pieces on ice in an insulated cooler, dash right home and cook them immediately. Make sure the fish guy gives you the upper shells intact because once the tomalley has been cooked and removed, the bright orange upper shells can be rinsed and used as serving dishes for this paella or vegetables and garnishes.

INGREDIENTS:

2 live crabs
2 large tomatoes, cut in chunks
¼ tsp saffron, rubbed
1 cup uncooked rice
2 cups stock, wine or water
salt, pepper to taste

Yields **3-4** servings

1. On a shallow dish, place crab shells upside down and arrange separated crab legs on top. Steam in the top of a steamer over rapidly boiling water for 10 minutes. Remove to cool. Scrape the tomalley out of crab shells and reserve. Drain off any water that has collected in the dish during the cooking process. Set this crab water aside to use as part of the liquid used to cook the rice. Using nutcrackers or the back of a cleaver, crack shell of front pincer legs and set aside whole. Crack meat-filled carapace apart and pick meat from back legs and body and season with salt to taste. If necessary, use heavy scissors to cut open the shells so you can pull out the meat. Discard empty shells.

2. In a paella pan or very large frying pan with lid, add oil over medium heat. Add garlic and cook gently until translucent. Add tomatoes, rice, liquid (including reserved crab water), saffron and boil until liquid level is the same as rice level. For this pilaf, basmati rice is best, but any long-grain rice will work. Place lid on tightly and cook for 20-30 more minutes or until rice is tender, then remove lid and add half of the tomalley (or none, if you hate it) and layer crabmeat on top. Place pincer claws on top of all. Replace lid and cook for another 5 minutes or just until crab is heated through. Remove from heat, stir to distribute crabmeat evenly. Salt to taste. Transfer to serving dish and arrange the pincer claws on top. Serve with chopped green onions and a sauce made from the remaining tomalley by pureeing it with an immersion blender in equal parts with mayonnaise.

PAELLA ON THE ROCKS

Hannibal used crabmeat for the paella he served to Tobias, stuffing the flavourful rice back into the crab shell for the presentation in *Fromage,* season 1, episode 7. Here is a variation you can cook on the beach: Paella cooked *aire libre*. Take your groceries outside into the summer's evening light and try it. Add sangria and it will be a memorable meal to share with your squad!

INGREDIENTS:

1 lb clams in shells scrubbed clean

½ lb mussels in shells scrubbed clean

1 cooked chicken leg, boned, cut in chunks

1 Tbsp olive oil

2 cloves garlic, minced

2-3 tomatoes, cut into chunks

¼ tsp saffron, rubbed

1 cup uncooked rice

2 cups stock, wine or water

salt, pepper to taste

Yields **4** servings

1. Make the fire's perimeter out of several large rocks of the same height, or use an iron tripod that can provide level support for your paella pan (or deep sauté pan with a lid).

2. Build a wood fire under the pan.

3. When the flames are licking hotly at the sides of the pan, add oil, garlic, tomatoes, clams and mussels. Throw in that glass of wine you've been drinking and cover. Simmer until mussels and clams are just cooked, removing them from the pan with a slotted spoon and transferring them to a mixing bowl as soon as the shells open. Mussels will open first and fast. Clams take longer – be patient. Set cooked seafood aside.

4. To the pan, add the rice and saffron plus enough liquid (water, stock, wine, Bloody Caesar) to equal 2 cups. Allow all to boil gently. If mixture is boiling too rapidly, spread the wood away from the centre of the fire. Boil until the top of the liquid is level with the top of the rice.

5. Scoop out all flaming wood under the pan to lower the temperature, stir rice quickly and cover tightly. Continue cooking until rice is tender (25-35 min). Return seafood to the pan along with cooked chicken and cover. Cook just until hot.

MOLLY'S TROUT (309)

So easy it can be made over a campfire by the lake, the buttery crunch of the oatmeal makes this trout preparation simple but special. Molly makes this for dinner when Jack comes to take away her Will.

INGREDIENTS:

Four 10-12 oz rainbow trout, gutted, scaled, gills and fin bones removed
1 egg
½ cup milk
½ cup flour
1½ cups rolled oats
½ cup butter
salt, pepper to taste
lemon wedges

Yields dinner for **4**

1. In a large plate or pie pan, beat egg together with milk. Set aside. In another large plate, spread out oatmeal. Dredge a trout with flour, dip it into the egg mixture on both sides and roll in oatmeal, coating both sides well. Set aside and repeat with remaining trout.

2. Melt a tablespoon of the butter in a large sauté pan over medium-high heat. When butter begins to bubble, add trout to pan. Cook in several batches to avoid crowding pan. Cook on one side until golden brown, turn over, add another tablespoon of butter and cook other side until golden brown and fish flakes off the bone when forked (about 5 minutes each side). While sautéing, add more butter to pan if it goes dry. Season with salt and pepper to taste. Arrange on platter, garnish with lemon wedges and serve.

TRUITE AU BLEU ENGASTRA (206)

Truite au bleu is one of those dishes that comes to mind when classic French cuisine is mentioned. To make it, you must start with live trout because the part of the fish that turns blue — pale grey, really — is the mucus that coats the living fish. So you must handle the fish as little as possible so as not to rub away the mucus. The skin is not eaten — it's full of scales. It can be peeled away before serving or left on so the "bleu" can be seen by the diners, but then you should remind your guests not to eat the skin.

If you can't get live trout, you can still make it this style but you might not get any "bleu" effect.

INGREDIENTS:

four 8 oz whole trout, gutted
4 qt court bouillon
1 cup wine vinegar
2 cups hot fish bouillon or vegetable broth

Yields **4** servings

For the court bouillon, fill the fish poacher three-quarters full of water, add ½ tsp salt per cup of water, rough cut carrots, celery, halved onion, bay leaves and lemon slices. Bring to boil and reduce heat to simmer.

1. Handling the trout as little a possible, slit the belly open all the way from the collar bone to the anus and open the abdomen, spreading the sides out flat. Put the needle-nose pliers through the mouth and grab the tail. Gently but firmly pull the tail through the mouth as far as you can, folding the trout over itself. The teeth should keep the tail from sliding back.

2. Put the folded trout on a square of parchment and place it in a bowl. Add the vinegar and spoon it over the trout until the mucus on the skin coating turns pale bluish-white. Using the parchment to lift it, remove trout from vinegar bath and lower into court bouillon ensuring that the fish is completely immersed in the broth. Repeat with remaining trout. Poach gently for 6 to 8 minutes. Remove fish from court bouillon with lifter or large slotted spoon. Drain and transfer to soup plate. Peel off and discard the skin from body of the trout if you wish, but leave the skin of the tail, head and neck intact — this is where most of the "bleu" will show. Slide away the parchment and discard. At the table, ladle ½ cup broth into each bowl over the fish. Serve with Hollandaise sauce.

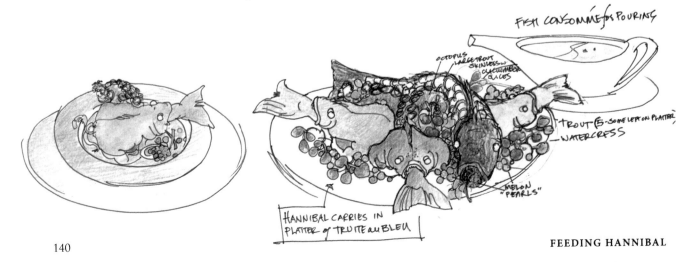

FISH CONSOMMÉ for POURING

octopus
LARGE TROUT
SKINLESS w
CUCUMBER
SLICES

TROUT (5 - SOME LEFT ON PLATTER
WATERCRESS

MELON
"PEARLS"

HANNIBAL CARRIES IN
PLATTER of TRUITE au BLEU

EPISODE 2.12 TOME-WAN   SC11   HANNIBAL UNMOULDS KHOLODETS
                                       FOR JACK

A **ZAKUSKI** DINNER
FEATURING ANCHOVETA KHOLODETS

KHOLODETS WITH MOBIUS STRIP of
    ANCHOVETAS IN CLEAR GELATINE

SHREDDED MEAT & VEG
    IN BASE of
    KHOLODETS

LARGE SHARDS
    OF
    KHOLODETS

SMALL
SHARDS
of
GELÉE

GARNISH of
HERBS +
BABY APPLES

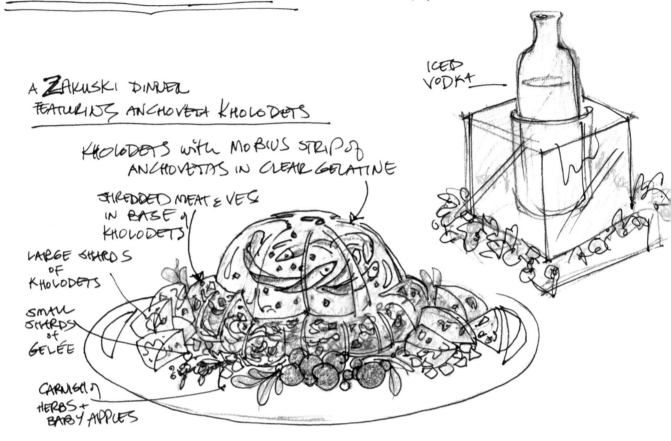

ICED
VODKA

CAVIAR PLATTER

STARGAZY PIE

SHELLS of TRI COLOUR CAVIAR on ICE
    SALMON, GOLDEN & BLACK
                with
        MINI BLINIS

STURGEON HEAD PIE from
GOGOL'S "DEAD SOULS"
(ZAKUSKI DINNER of POLICE CHIEF)

KHOLODETS (212)

To make an authentic Kholodets you must simmer a large whole stewing chicken in water with onion and carrot for several hours until all the meat has fallen off the bones. The jelly of a really elegant Kholodets is almost clear and meltingly soft. It's delicately delicious but often too soft to hold its shape once it is turned out of the mould.

This recipe calls for veal shanks and pork hocks, which have much more cartilage and as a result will gel more solidly and unmould more easily. The result will be much more firm.

INGREDIENTS:

3 pig's trotters, scrubbed clean, bristles removed

1 lb veal shank

1 lb chicken thighs

1 large carrot

1 medium onion

1 tsp pickling spice mix*

salt, pepper to taste

½ cup diced carrots, cooked

½ cup peas, cooked

*Pickling Spice is available premixed but you can substitute 4 parts coriander, 2 part peppercorns, 2-3 bay leaves, 1 part cloves, 1 part cinnamon stick.

Yields Main dish for **6** or Appetizer for **12**

1. In a large stock pot, over high heat, place trotters, shanks, thighs, carrot and onion quarters, pickling spice mix and 3 to 4 quarts of water (enough to cover meat) and bring to a boil. Turn heat down and allow to simmer for 5-6 hours or until meat falls off the bone and skin and cartilage are very soft. The liquid should be reduced by half. Skim of any coagulated foam that forms on the top of the liquid.

2. Remove bones and large pieces of meat. Strain stock through a fine sieve and discard vegetables and bones. Chop meat in ½" dice, mix with diced cooked carrots and peas, season with salt and pepper and place into large mould or 2 loaf pans. Pour over strained stock. Chill until solid – at least 3 hours or overnight if possible. When ready to serve, dip mould in very hot water until a thin layer of jelly melts around the perimeter. Wiggle the mould to see if the jelly has loosened from all sides. Invert and unmould onto a platter, slice and serve with horseradish and apologies.

MOBIUS FISH IN ASPIC

Kholodets was without doubt the most mocked meal I ever made for Hannibal. The Season 2 blooper reel reveals Laurence Fishburne's "gag" about it. So, for your *Tome-wan* rewatch dinners, I created this substitute. It's an elegant dish inspired by the anchovy diorama that Hannibal stages in the aspic of his Kholodets. Served cold, it's lovely on a hot summer's night: filets of pink and white fish braided into a colourful twist and suspended in aspic with a mosaic of vegetables.

INGREDIENTS:

For fish twist:
Two 6-oz filets of sole, skinless, boneless
One 6-oz filet of Arctic char, skinless, boneless
2 Tbsp butter, melted
½ tsp Italian herb mix or fines herbes
¼ tsp salt

For aspic:
4 cups vegetable stock
2 Tbsp unflavoured gelatin
2 Tbsp cold water or white wine
¾ cup mixed diced vegetables, frozen
¼ tsp lemon juice
1 tsp chopped fresh dill weed
salt and pepper to taste

Yields **2** main servings.

1. Prepare fish: The Arctic char and the sole should be very similar in size and shape. Cut the Arctic char in two equal halves lengthwise along the backbone line. Set aside. Split the two filets of sole down the middle, leaving the two halves attached at the wide end of the filet. Set one aside. Place one strip of Arctic Char between the two halves of one of the filets of sole. Weave over and back, braiding the three strips together. Repeat with the other pieces of fish.

2. In a small bowl, combine melted butter with herb mix and salt. Set aside. Line a 2-cup soup-bowl with a large piece of plastic food wrap, Arrange one of the fish braids inside the lined bowl, pushing the fish to the sides of the bowl. Place a 1½" diameter biscuit cutter or ball of crumpled aluminum foil in the middle of the bowl to hold the braided fish against the bottom and sides of the bowl. Bring up sides of plastic wrap tightly over the fish and tuck into biscuit cutter or twist together at the top to hold fish in shape. Repeat with the second braid of fish. Place bowls in steamer over boiling water and cook for 8-10 minutes. Remove and pour off any liquid. When cool enough to handle, invert on a plate to drain off any remaining liquid. Pat dry with paper towels. Refrigerate for at least 1 hour.

3. Prepare aspic. In a small saucepan, bring stock to boil. In a small dish, sprinkle gelatin over cold water or white wine and allow gelatin to moisten. Remove stock from heat and add gelatin. Stir until gelatin has melted completely. Stir in dill, lemon juice and frozen vegetables. Season to taste.

4. Wash and dry steaming bowls and line with plastic wrap. Remove plastic wrap from steamed fish and place each back in a bowl in original position. Remove biscuit cutters or foil. Spoon aspic into bowls, putting most of the vegetables in the cavity in the middle of the fish braid. Add enough aspic to cover the top of the fish. Refrigerate for at least 4 hours. When ready to serve, invert each onto a plate. Lift off bowls, peel off plastic wrap and serve with Honey Mustard Cream (p153) and your favorite potato salad.

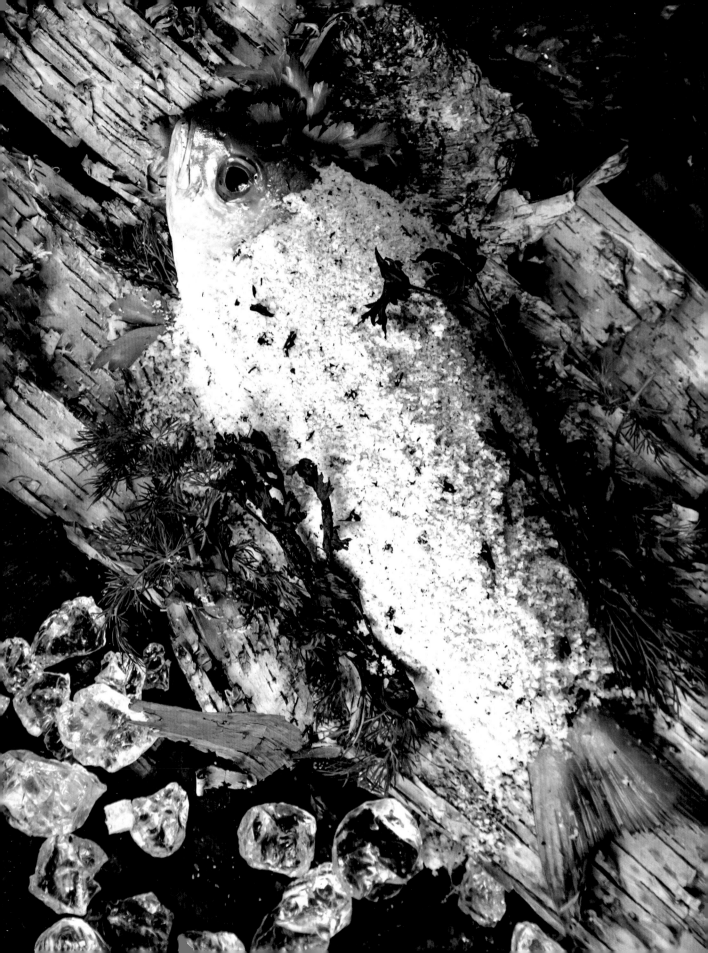

Ash-Salt Baked Snapper (201)

In *Antipasto,* Helpful Hannibal serves Dr Chilton an Ash-Salt Baked Celeriac – an easily digestible vegetarian dinner – out of consideration for his recent kidney loss. Assuming Hannibal has not stolen your kidney, here's a fish recipe that uses the same principle: a thick shell of salt creates a dry, airtight insulated jacket so the contents will bake gently and evenly in their own steam. The scales also help keep the moisture in, so don't scale the fish and when you serve the fish, remove and discard the skin after you break away the salt. One fish serves one person, just add a tossed green salad or roasted vegetables.

Ingredients:

7 cups medium grind salt such as
    kosher or grey sea salt
¾ cup crushed ash*
2 egg whites
3 Tbsp water

two 1-1¼ lb whole fish such as red
    snapper, branzino or trout, gutted,
    but not scaled
½ bunch fresh parsley
2 thick lemon or orange slices, halved
    into semi-circles
4 Tbsp olive oil

* You can buy ash at gourmet stores but it's easy to make your own. Roast vegetable off-cuts like celery and carrot tops, corn husks and potato peelings in the oven at 350°F for 1½-2 hours until they are completely dried out and burnt black. Leafy celery tops will curl up and scorch to look like stag horns – a great garnish! You don't need much – just one baking sheet of charred vegetables will be enough to crumble and add to the salt to give your baked fish a smoky accent.

Yields 2 main servings

1. In a bowl, mix together salt and crushed ash. Set aside.

2. In a medium-sized mixing bowl, whisk egg white til frothy. Add water and whisk til combined. Add ¾ of it to salt mixture. Mix thoroughly til all the salt is damp and clingy – like sand when you are making a sand castle. To test consistency, take a couple tablespoonsful in your palm and make a fist, crushing salt together. When you open your hand, salt should stay clumped with some cracking. If not, add more egg-water a bit at a time to the salt mixture until it holds together. Don't add too much egg white or it will be a struggle to crack the salt shell once it's baked. Set aside.

3. Preheat oven to 400°F. Line a small baking sheet with a sheet of baking parchment and place about 1½ cup of salt mixture in the middle. Spread out to the approximate length and width of your fish. Tamp down to a ½" thickness. Using paper towel, dry one fish off then rub skin and cavity with olive oil and place on top of the salt. Stuff cavity with lemon slices and herbs. Spoon about 1½ cups of the salt mixture on top and sides, pressing over the fish so the fish is encased in a ½" layer of salt while taking care to not get salt inside the fish cavity. You can leave the head and tail exposed if you wish. Repeat with second fish.

4. Roast for 20-25 minutes. Remove from oven and rest for 10 minutes. Transfer to a wooden cutting board or individual platters and serve.

5. To serve: At the table, crack the salt shell by tapping gently with a mallet or the heel of a chef's knife handle, then push aside the salt shards, brushing salt bits away from the fish or they will make the fish too salty. Pull away the top layer of skin, using a sharp thin knife to detach the skin from the gill, fins, and tail. Using a wide fork, lift the meat off the bones and serve onto individual plates. When the top side has been served, remove the bone by lifting the head up and away toward the tail. All the small bones will come away with the spine. Remove the fin bones and serve the bottom half of the fish meat, leaving the skin on the salt crust. Have a martini—you deserve it.

IS NOTHING HERE VEGETARIAN?

No matter how many times Hannibal and Will have dinner together, it ends with unresolved feelings. Here amid the platters of honeycombs and walnuts, pomegranates and figs, Will sits, catatonic. Hannibal, bruised but unbended, doggedly brings out his skull saw and goes for his main course.

Will's brain has turned to food.

When we were shooting this, the saw blade fell off a few times – but Mads performed retakes with aplomb, never compromising the tension of the scene. Even with Laurence at the other end of the table, alternately screaming and laughing for his takes.

Here are a couple of vegetarian presentations to consider while Hannibal revs up the exquisite little oscillating saw that he keeps in a box beside the gravy ladle.

Vegetarian Osso Buco

Ingredients:

2 large eggplant

3 leeks

1 carrot cut in ¼" dice

6 Tbsp olive oil

1 tsp Italian or Provençal herb mix

5 plum tomatoes

Balsamic glaze, optional

Yields **2-3** main course servings

1. Remove ends from eggplants and cut each cross-wise into 3 discs 3-4" thick. Using a small paring knife, pierce a small "x" in the middle of each disc all the way through. Set aside. Trim green tops and root end from leeks. Cut two 4" lengths from the white part of each leek. Wash well and set aside. Reserve green offcuts for use at another time. Cut tomatoes into 1-inch dice. Set aside.

2. Over medium-high heat, add 2 Tbsp oil to Dutch oven or lidded frying pan large enough to hold eggplant slices in one layer. Add eggplant slices and sauté on both sides until slightly softened and beginning to brown, adding oil as needed. Transfer to cookie sheet. Add 1 Tbsp oil to Dutch oven and add leeks and carrots. Sauté until slightly softened, turning to brown all sides. Remove leeks to a bowl. Heat 1 Tbsp oil in Dutch oven and add tomatoes and herbs. Arrange eggplant slices on top and push one length of leek into the X in the middle of each eggplant slice. It should stand upright, like the bone of a piece of osso buco. Cover and reduce heat to low, simmering gently for 10-15 minutes or until eggplant is cooked through but firm enough to hold it's shape. Check occasionally to make sure tomatoes are not going dry or burning. Add water or reduce heat further if necessary. Season with salt and pepper to taste and arrange on platter. Drizzle with Balsamic glaze if desired.

CAULIFLOWER PEAS PILAF

Here's a no-grain, no shellfish version of paella. It substitutes cauliflower for rice which makes this a great dish for anyone avoiding grains, carbs and seafood.

INGREDIENTS:

½ head cauliflower
2 Tbsp coconut oil or butter
½ onion, cut in ¼" dice
1 rib celery, cut in ¼" dice
2 cloves garlic, chopped
½ cup peas
3 green onions, chopped
4 oz ground chicken, pork or lamb
¼ tsp cumin, crushed
1 tsp curry powder or smoked paprika
¼ cup flat leaf parsley, chopped
1 cup chicken stock
salt and pepper to taste

Yields **4** main course servings,
8 side dish servings

1. Cut florets off cauliflower and set aside. Cut stems into 1" chunks. place in food processor fitted with chopping blade and run for 1 minute or until pieces are the size of rice kernels. Transfer to bowl and set aside. Add half of the florets to processor and pulse 3 or 4 times until florets have crumbled to rice-sized pieces. Transfer to bowl of chopped stems. Repeat with remaining florets. Set aside.

2. Heat 1 Tbsp oil in large deep skillet over medium-high heat. Add onions and fry for a few moments. Add celery and garlic and fry until onions are translucent and celery is tender. Transfer to bowl and set aside.

3. Return skillet to heat and add the remaining oil, cumin, curry and the ground meat. Fry, tossing to crumble meat as it cooks. Add parsley and fry until meat is cooked through. Add cooked vegetables, peas, cauliflower and chicken stock. Bring to boil and cover. Allow to boil for 2-3 minutes or until stock has reduced and cauliflower is tender but still firm. Add salt and pepper to taste. Remove from heat and serve.

RATATOUILLE

This easy vegetable stew is light but full of flavour and colour and great served over Faux Foie Torchon (p76). It is also very versatile: you can add olives, summer squash or green peppers. If you don't have an Italian mix on your spice shelf, use equal parts of dried rubbed oregano, basil, rosemary and thyme.

INGREDIENTS:

3 Tbsp olive oil
1 onion, cut in 1-inch dice
1 small eggplant, cut in 1" cubes
1 zucchini, cut in ½" dice
2-3 cloves garlic, crushed
1 red bell pepper, cut in 1" chunks
1 yellow bell pepper cut in 1" chunks
5 tomatoes, rough chopped
1 tsp Italian mix herbs
salt and pepper to taste

Yields **3** main servings or
6 appetizers with Faux Foie

1. In a casserole or heavy skillet with lid, heat the oil over medium heat. Add onions and sauté until they begin to turn translucent, add eggplant and sauté, stirring constantly until they begin to brown. Add zucchini, garlic, bell peppers and cook until zucchini begins to turn translucent. Add tomatoes and herbs and reduce heat to low. Cover and simmer until vegetables are tender (about 30 minutes). Add salt and pepper to taste and serve over slices of Faux Foie Torchon (p76) or with Snail Pesto Buns (p170) or garlic toast.

HONEY MUSTARD CREAM

INGREDIENTS:

¼ cup mayonnaise
2 tsp honey mustard*
¼ cup whipping cream

substitute for honey mustard: 3 parts mustard, 1 part sugar

Yields **¾** cup of sauce

1. In a bowl, beat whipping cream with electric beater or French whip until firm peaks form. Set aside.

2. In a second bowl, mix mayonnaise and mustard together until completely blended. Add whipped cream and with a large rubber spatula, fold together gently just until well-blended. Refrigerate until ready to serve.

VEGETARIAN PUMPKIN LASAGNA AL DENTURES

At Grandmother Dolarhyde's boarding house, the food was so mushy that you didn't need to put your false teeth in for dinner. Perhaps that's one reason why Francis feared teeth so – he wasn't used to seeing them outside the denture box. Well, that and getting chomped on by Granny.

When we filmed the boarding house dinner scene, the food had to look grey and flat so I had to present the dishes ungarnished but I couldn't resist throwing in a few loose teeth – giant white corn, sold in cans as hominy, did the trick!

To cook the pumpkin, cut in wedges, scoop out seeds and steam for 15 minutes or until flesh is fork-tender. Remove and discard the peel.

INGREDIENTS:

1½ lb fresh pasta sheets or 12-16 pc
   dried lasagna sheets
olive oil

1 onion, diced
4 cups pumpkin, cubed and cooked
¼ cup butter
3 stems fresh sage
½ cup whipping cream
salt, pepper to taste

8 oz chèvre
8 oz ricotta cheese
1 egg, beaten
1 bunch spinach

4 cups prepared tomato sauce
½ cup hominy corn, optional
2 cup grated Fontina cheese or other
   mild melting cheese like Jack or
   mozzarella
½ cup grated Parmesan cheese

Yields **6** servings

1. Make the pumpkin filling: In a heavy-bottomed saucepan, heat butter over medium-low heat. Add diced onions and sage and cook slowly until onions are translucent and pale gold. Remove sage. Add cooked pumpkin and cream and mash together in pan until heated through. Season with salt and pepper to taste. Remove from heat and set aside.

2. Make the spinach-chèvre layer: Cut off and discard root end of spinach clusters to separate leaves. Wash well then shake off excess water and put leaves into a zippered plastic freezer bag. Zip partly closed, leaving 2" open for steam to escape. Microwave for 1½ minutes or until wilted. Allow to cool before opening the bag. Drain, chop roughly and set aside. In a mixing bowl, crumble chèvre and ricotta. Add spinach. Season with salt and pepper to taste. Add egg and mix together. Set aside.

3. Prepare the pasta pot: Bring a large pot of salted water to boil over medium heat.

4. Assemble lasagna: In a baking pan about 9" x 12" x 3"deep, brush olive oil liberally on bottom and sides. Into the pot of boiling water, add enough lasagna sheets to cover bottom and sides of baking dish. Cook for 1 minute then remove with tongs or slotted spoon and transfer to prepared baking pan and arrange in a single layer. Spread on half of the tomato sauce and sprinkle with half of the grated Fontina.

5. Par-boil and add another layer of lasagna sheets and spread on half of the pumpkin mixture. Add another layer of par-boiled lasagna sheets, the chevre mixture, a layer of boiled lasagna sheets, the rest of the pumpkin, a layer of boiled lasagna sheets and the rest of the tomato sauce.

6. Sprinkle with Parmesan and the rest of the grated Fontina and if you wish, hominy "teeth". Cover very loosely with foil and bake in a preheated oven at 325°F for 40 minutes. Remove foil and bake an additional 20 minutes to brown cheese. Cut in squares and serve.

HAVING FRIENDS
FOR DINNER

SOUPS, SALADS
AND SIDE DISHES

SILKIE CHICKEN SOUP
WITH WOLFBERRIES

When Will was in hospital, Hannibal fed him this ancient Asian remedy of exotic ingredients in a broth made from Silkie chicken, a Chinese breed of poultry. This unusual bird has a fluffy coat of long white silky feathers that contrast starkly with its blue-black skin, black bones and lean dark flesh.

The flavourful broth is enriched with nutritious wolfberries (Goji berries). These small dried red berries can be found in Asian grocery stores and health food stores. If you want to give your broth an Asian accent, add fresh ginger, red dates, fresh peanuts, dried longan and white snow fungus; they add earthy herbal flavours as well as restorative nutrients.

INGREDIENTS:

one 2½ lb Silkie chicken, cut in 6-8
   pieces
1 onion, diced
3 plum tomatoes, diced
½ oz dried wolfberries
1 carrot, diced
½ cup fresh green peas
salt, pepper to taste

Yields **4** servings

1. In a heat-proof bowl, pour boiling water over chicken pieces and let it sit for 5 minutes. Drain hot water off and rinse chicken with cold water, brushing away any coagulated blood or bits of liver that cling to the bones.

2. In a large stockpot, cover chicken pieces with cold water and bring to boil, skimming off any foam that forms on the surface. Reduce heat and simmer for 4 to 6 hours adding water as necessary to keep chicken pieces covered in liquid. If you are adding any dried Chinese herbs such as red dates, fresh peanuts or dried longan, rinse them well and add them now with a small piece of ginger.

3. Thirty minutes before serving, take chicken pieces out of the broth, remove and discard bones, skin, head, neck, wings and feet. Skim off any foam that has collected on the surface of the broth. Add boiling water if necessary so you have about 4 cups of broth. Cut chicken meat into ½" dice. Return diced chicken to pot of simmering broth and add wolfberries, onions, carrots, peas and tomatoes. If you are using white fungus, rinse it well under cold water and add it now. Simmer for 20 minutes and season to taste with salt and pepper. Serve in small bowls.

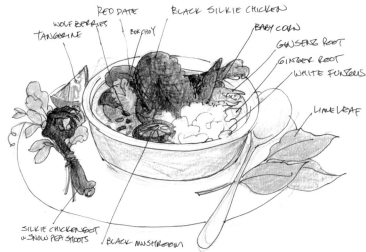

CHILLED TOMATO PLASMA CONSOMMÉ (107)

Preparing dinner for his opera-going frenemies, Hannibal cheerfully centrifuges blood to capture the clear plasma that he will make into soup. "They will love the sweet flavour," he tells Will who has dropped by to say he can't drop by.

Just as sweet and just as clear, but not requiring people-blood, here is a wonderful tomato consommé as colourless and cold as Hannibal's own plasma.

INGREDIENTS:

For the clear plasma:
6 medium-sized ripe field tomatoes
1 rib of celery, chopped
2 shallots, peeled and rough chopped
5-6 leaves fresh basil
½ tsp maple syrup or sugar
salt, pepper to taste

For garnish:
2 cherry tomatoes, cut into flower or
   rose (p216)
2 sprigs of fresh basil
balsamic vinegar and olive oil to drizzle

Yields 2 servings

1. Remove and discard stems and sepals of field tomatoes and rough cut into large chunks. In a food processer, combine tomato chunks, celery, shallots and pulse off/on 5 or 6 times until chopped and frothy.

2. In a large heavy-bottomed pot, heat tomato mixture over high heat until it comes to a boil. Add basil, maple syrup, salt and pepper and reduce heat to low. Simmer for 30 minutes.

3. Gently pour tomato mixture to large strainer fitted over a bowl. When the flow of liquid through the strainer slows, transfer the strainer and its contents to a clean bowl to continue dripping. Strain the liquid from the first bowl through another large strainer that is lined with a large paper coffee filter or a square of paper towel. Allow both strainers to drip until no more liquid is exuded – about 15 minutes. If the liquid in either bowl has any red traces, strain through paper filter again. Discard tomato pulp and filters. Combine clear liquid and adjust seasonings. Transfer into a lidded container and refrigerate until ready to serve.

4. Prepare soup bowls by dividing cherry tomato and basil sprigs equally between the bowls and then filling with tomato liquid. Garnish with a few drops each of vinegar and olive oil. Serve with anchovies and olives on toast.

ROASTED CAULIFLOWER BRAIN (111)

Always thoughtful about balancing his meals, Hannibal serves a platter of Roasted Cauliflower Brains to Chilton as a side dish to his Curried Sheep Intestines. He rubbed one cauliflower with red tandoori spice the other with yellow curry spices.

This recipe calls for Mimolette cheese, which I used a lot for Hannibal because I love its rich orange colour and plump ball shape. You can substitute any grating cheese such as Parmesan Reggiano or Crotonese. The Caper Berry Drizzle is optional but it's a Hannibal favourite—he makes it in Season 3's episode 6 as he prepares to sauté Will's brain.

INGREDIENTS:

1 whole cauliflower head
4-5 Tbsp olive oil
smoked paprika and salt to taste
¼ cup grated Mimolette cheese

Caper Berry Drizzle:
¼ cup butter
1 Tbsp caper berries, chopped
1 Tbsp shallots, minced
1 tsp lemon juice

Yields **4-6** side servings

1. Cut stem and lower leaves off so cauliflower sits upright in pan without tipping. Using a sharp paring knife cut a deep X into the core from the bottom. (This will allow the core to cook more quickly.)

2. Place cauliflower on a rectangle of cooking parchment or foil large enough to wrap the whole head and slowly pour olive oil all over cauliflower, turning it upside down to get oil in the stem side as well as the top and sides, and rubbing oil into all the florets. Sprinkle salt and smoked paprika over whole surface of cauliflower. Bring sides of parchment up and fold the ends under, enclosing the cauliflower. Place this package in a shallow pan. Roast at 375°F for 45 minutes. Open up package, brush with more olive oil and sprinkle cheese on top and roast, uncovered, for an additional 30-40 minutes or until tender and browned.

3. Make drizzle: In a sauté pan over medium heat, combine butter and shallots. Sauté, stirring frequently, until shallots are tender and translucent. Add caper berries and lemon juice. Stir to combine and heat through. Drizzle over roasted cauliflower.

SORTA CAESAR DRESSING

For those who are ambivalent about garlic breath and anchovies, this dressing replaces the hot tang of garlic with horseradish and the umami of anchovies with honey.

INGREDIENTS:

2 Tbsp mayonnaise
2 Tbsp olive oil
1 Tbsp lemon juice
1 tsp liquid honey
1 tsp horseradish

1. In a bowl, whisk all ingredients together. Drizzle a spoonful on each salad and serve the rest on the side for those who like more dressing.

ROAST TRYPOPHOBIA GARLIC

As well as being a creepy-looking but delicious garnish for your Caesar salads, this is great smeared on toast or incorporated into salad dressing. Just pull the garlic bulbs apart into separate cloves and squeeze the caramelized garlic out of each clove, discarding the papery shells. You can roast several bulbs at a time as they will keep frozen for several months.

INGREDIENTS:

2 large bulbs garlic
4 tsp olive oil

1. Preheat oven to 375°F. Slice top quarter off each garlic bulb so the top of each clove is exposed. Rub 2 tsp olive oil into the open cloves of each bulb. Place in the center of a piece of aluminum foil about 10" x 6" and gather up sides to completely enclose garlic. Place in oven on cookie sheet. Roast for 40-60 min. When garlic is fork-tender and browned, remove and cool.

Caesar Salad Bouquets (106)

When Hannibal lays a table, he can't resist toying with classics and putting his own improvements on things. Here's a way of presenting a Caesar salad so the leaves sprout up like a verdant fountain. You can make the salads in individual servings as directed, or, as Hannibal did in *Entrée* (season 1, episode 6) for Alana and Dr Chilton, place them together on a large platter surrounded by clusters of assorted mushrooms, vegetables and sprouts, like a miniature Villa D'Este landscape done in garden greens, replete with skull follies and watchful peacock tail eyes (p228).

INGREDIENTS:

For the bread rings and crisps
1 baguette or 1 slice of tramezzini*
4 Tbsp butter

For the salad
14-18 leaves 4-6" long, from hearts of
    romaine
2 oz Parmesan or other hard cheese
    thinly shaved
¼ cup Caesar salad dressing (prepared,
    or recipe on p163)
4 to 6 rolled anchovies, optional
½ whole roasted garlic, optional (recipe
    on p163)

*tramezzini is soft white crustless
sandwich loaf cut lengthwise to yield
long rectangular slices perfect for making
rolled party sandwiches.*

Yields **2** servings,

1. To prepare bread rings, cut ends off baguette to make a 12" length. Set aside ends for another use. Using a long slicing knife or a serrated bread knife, and holding the loaf segment on its side, slice off the bottom crust, then cut the rest lengthwise in 3 slices. Set aside the top and bottom crust slices for use at another time. Trim side crusts from the middle two slices and discard crusts. Or if you are using a slice of tramezzini, cut it in half lengthwise. You should have 2 crustless slices about ½" x 2" x 12". Flatten slices slightly with a rolling pin. Brush both sides of with melted butter. Preheat oven or toaster oven to 350°F.

2. To shape the crouton rings, wrap one crustless slice loosely around a 2" diameter biscuit cutter, or wadded-up foil and fasten closed with toothpicks. Not too snugly, as bread will shrink while it toasts. Repeat with the other slice and bake until golden-brown, about 10 minutes. When cool enough to handle, carefully slide toasted rings off biscuit cutters. Set aside to cool and dry completely.

3. To compose the salad, gather half of the romaine leaves, stem side down, into a little bouquet and put an elastic band around the cluster about 3" from the bottom. Slice the ends off so the stem ends are even. Squeeze together the bottom of the cluster and slide into a bread ring until the cut ends emerge from the other side of the ring. Using scissors, snip off the elastic band. Stand the cluster upright on the plate and fan the leaves out to balance it so it stands up without tipping over. Repeat with the remaining leaves and bread ring. Place each cluster in the middle of a plate. Drizzle salad dressing and scatter Parmesan shavings around the edge of the plate along with several rolled anchovies and 3-6 cloves of roasted garlic (recipe on p163).

QUINOA TABOULEH

B ased on the classic middle-eastern favourite, tabouleh, this nutritious salad uses quinoa instead of cracked bulgur. It makes a great accompaniment to Kibbeh Tongues (p102) or Roasted Marrow Bones (p70). For Hannibal, I loved using black quinoa because it looks like dirt teeming with tiny worms.

INGREDIENTS:

1 cup cooked quinoa
1 cup chopped parsley
1 Tbsp lemon juice
1 Tbsp olive oil
1 Tbsp mint sauce

Yields **2-3** servings

1. 1 In a small bowl, combine lemon juice, olive oil and mint sauce. Add quinoa and toss to mix well. Add parsley, toss and serve.

CANDIED GINGER

U se in salads, or for cookies and muffins, or dip in chocolate to make fantastic candies. When you are making this candied ginger, save the cooking liquid to make ginger tea.

INGREDIENTS:

1-2 large pieces ginger root, about ½ lb
1 cup sugar for syrup
½ cup sugar for coating

1. Peel and slice ginger into coins about ⅛" thick. Bring 2 cups water to boil in heavy-bottomed saucepan over high heat. Add sliced ginger and reduce heat to low. Simmer for 30 minutes until ginger has softened but is still a bit crispy. Pour off water, reserving it. Add sugar and ½ cup of the reserved cooking liquid. Return to heat stir together boil very gently. When foam builds up, lower heat. Continue simmering on low until liquid is syrupy and ginger has darkened and become translucent, about 45 minutes. Remove from heat.

2. Using tongs, remove the ginger pieces from the syrup and place in a single layer on a wire cookie rack to drain. Allow to drip dry 3-4 hours. Place sugar in a plastic food bag and add the ginger. Close top of the bag and shake until all ginger is coated. Remove ginger slices from bag, shaking off excess sugar. Allow to air-dry for 1-2 days then store in a dry, airtight container.

Blood Orange Treviso Salad (304)

Treviso…that most Hannibal of salad greens, is gorgeous yet ominous – its pigeon-blood ruby colour contrasting starkly with its white stalks and veins – like old blood seeping across sparkling new snow.

Ingredients:

1 head treviso
1 small head frisée or baby salad greens
2 blood oranges, sliced, unpeeled
½ red onion, thinly sliced

Yields **3-4** side servings

1. Holding treviso upright under the tap, run cold water into top of the treviso, so it forces the leaves to open like a huge flower, running your fingers between the leaves to help ease them apart. Place on platter and tuck orange and onion slices around and between leaves. Tuck clusters of frisée in and around the treviso to prop flower up on the plate.

2. Drizzle Beet Juice Vinaigrette (p170) over salad and serve.

FREDDIE'S GINGER CARROT-TOP SLAW (210)

Hannibal:"Will, you slice the ginger…"
Will:"I already have."

Happily for redhead Freddie Lounds, it's just ginger root, being sliced for dinner. Hannibal is being tricked by Will into thinking that they are dining on Freddie's flesh. Sadly for Will and Freddie, Dr Lecter is never fooled for very long.

For the scene, I made carrot slaw to represent Freddie's head on a plate like John the Baptist; long strands of carrot flowing from a quilled sea urchin the colour of Freddie's hat. I garnished the hat with giant porcupine quills – a culinary clue that Freddie, the journalist, will survive: the quill is mightier than the sword.

You need a special tool – a mandoline – to shred the carrots into long "hairs" but if you don't have one, just grate the carrots and say Freddie had a bad hair day.

INGREDIENTS:

2 Tbsp white balsamic vinegar
¼ tsp freshly grated ginger
1 tsp sugar
2 Tbsp liquid coconut oil
4 large carrots, peeled
1 Tbsp candied ginger, finely chopped
  (or other candied fruit)
salt and pepper to taste
edible flowers (optional)

Yields about **3** servings

1. In a medium-sized bowl, combine the vinegar, grated ginger and olive oil and whisk until smooth. Set aside.

2. Using a mandoline fitted with the vertical spiked blade for thin julienne and the slicing blade set at the low to very thin level, shred carrots lengthwise, pulling carrots their full length across the blade so the resulting shreds are as long as possible and resemble orange spaghetti. Don't try to slice the carrots all the way down or you risk cutting your fingers! Reserve the unsliced carrot for another use.

3. Fluff the carrot shreds apart and add them to the vinegar mixture, tossing to completely coat all the carrot shreds. To serve, swirl the carrot slaw on the platter like flowing curls of hair and decorate with edible flowers in the shape of a flower crown.

BEET JUICE VINAIGRETTE

INGREDIENTS:

1 cup beet juice
3 Tbsp olive oil
2 Tbsp white wine vinegar
½ tsp orange peel, grated
salt, pepper to taste

Yields ½ cup

1. In a small saucepan over medium heat, boil beet juice until reduced to ⅓ cup. Remove from heat. Add vinegar and oil and whisk together. Add salt and pepper to taste. Drizzle over endive greens.

SNAIL PESTO BUNS

Made from pizza dough and pizza ingredients, these chewy little buns will delight. And nary a snail will be harmed. These make an excellent accompaniment to escargot – I made them for Gideon's meal of arm snails.

INGREDIENTS:

I pkg pizza dough (1½ lb)
2 Tbsp pesto
2 Tbsp tomato paste
4 Tbsp grated Parmesan cheese
olive oil

Makes 24 mini buns.

1. Thaw dough in its plastic bag and leave in a warm place until it doubles in size. Remove from bag and punch down. Prepare mini-muffin tins by dropping ⅛ tsp olive oil in each cup.

2. Divide dough in half and, working on a pastry board or clean countertop, spread dough out into two thin rectangles about 4"x14". If the dough starts to spring back and becomes difficult to stretch to size, let it rest for 10-15 minutes so the gluten relaxes.

3. Spread one rectangle with pesto and the other with tomato paste. Sprinkle cheese evenly over both. Roll up into a cylinder about 1" diameter by 14" long. Cut into ½" round slices. Put one slice, cut side up, into each cup of the mini-muffin tin. Brush the tops with olive oil, cover very lightly with a piece of plastic wrap and let it rise in a warm place for 1-1½ hours or until double in size. Remove plastic wrap gently. Bake in an oven preheated to 350°F for 10 minutes or until buns have lightly browned. Allow to cool and try not to eat them all at once.

CURRIED BEET AND MANGO SALAD

A rtistic and elegant Ettie Shuken was my assistant through some of my darkest moments feeding Hannibal: cleaning chicken skulls, gutting trout, stuffing blood sausages, painting peeled grapes. On the brighter side, her salad-making skills were a delight. Here is a delicious and beautiful composition she made to go with Chilton's south Indian dinner when Hannibal presented Curried Sheep Gut.

Select a sweet and crispy apple variety such as Mitsu, Fuji, Jonas Gold and a mango that is fully ripe but still firm. For beet greens, choose the smaller, tender leaves.

INGREDIENTS:

For the salad:

5 small beets

1 large mango

1 apple

1 Tbsp chives, finely minced

5 fresh mint leaves, rough chopped

salt and pepper, to taste

3 cups baby arugula

1 cup tender beet greens, rough
   chopped

For the dressing:

2 tsp medium-hot Indian curry paste

1 tsp lemon juice

1 tsp lemon zest

1 tsp honey

2 Tbsp apple cider vinegar

1 Tbsp Chinese Sweet Chili Sauce

Yields 4 servings,

1. Rinse beets and wrap in foil. In an oven preheated to 375°F, roast until tender (about 45 minutes). When beets can be easily pierced with a knife, cool, peel and cut into bite-sized pieces. Transfer beets into a bowl. Drizzle dressing over warm beets and toss. Add chives and mint.

2. Peel and cut mango and apple into bite-size pieces and add to beets. Toss gently just to mix and set aside.

3. Spread arugula and beet greens on serving platter, top with beet mixture and serve.

BEVERLY BEET PÂTÉ (205)

T he gorgeous glowing colours of red and gold beets of this pâté bleed together and are revealed when the finished pâté is sliced in cross-section. Just like poor beloved Beverly in Season 2's *Mukozuke* when Hannibal enclosed her in sheets of acrylic like a Damien Hirst art installation.

INGREDIENTS:

2-3 red beets, boiled, peeled and thinly
 sliced

3-4 yellow beets, boiled, peeled and
 thinly sliced

8 oz chèvre (fresh goat cheese), softened

8 oz cream cheese, softened

salt, pepper, chopped dill

Yields **1** small pâté

1. In a small bowl, combine chèvre and cream cheese and beat together until smooth and soft. Set aside.

2. Line a small loaf pan with plastic food wrap extending at least 4" beyond the sides and ends of the pan. Line the bottom with yellow beet slices. Over the beets, spread a layer of chèvre mixture, sprinkle with salt, pepper and dill. Add to the pan another layer of yellow beets and another layer of chèvre. Repeat with remaining yellow beets, seasonings, more chèvre, then continue layering with the red beets alternating with chèvre and ending with a layer of red beets. Bring the plastic wrap up and over the pâté. Cover the pâté with more plastic film and refrigerate overnight, covered with a small board or plate. Weight with a heavy food can placed on top of the board. When ready to serve, turn out of loaf pan, remove plastic film and cut in ½" slices while cold, revealing the lovely colours.

Siam Wookie Balls (306)

C ordell made these rice balls to accompany the pigtail fingers he made for Mason Verger. The chewy fragrant rice is just the right counterpoint to the rich gelatinous pigtails – rice balls are, after all, finger food. If you don't feel like rolling the rice into balls, you can just serve it in bowls with the sesame seeds sprinkled on top. Sweet rice is also called short grain, sticky or glutinous rice.

INGREDIENTS:

1½ cups sweet rice (short grain glutinous)
2 cups water

black and white sesame seeds, toasted

Serves **4** as an accompaniment

1. If using a rice cooker: Combine rice and water in a rice cooker and cook according to instructions. On stovetop: Combine rice and water in a small heavy saucepan with a tight-fitting lid. Place on medium-high heat and boil without stirring until half of the water has boiled away and you can see it bubbling just below the surface of the rice (about 8 minutes). Turn heat down immediately to low, cover with lid and cook for another 20-30 minutes or until rice is cooked through and water has been fully absorbed.

2. Let rice rest uncovered until cool enough to handle (about 10 minutes). Scoop out about ⅛ cup of rice and roll into a ball with hands moistened with water (the water will keep the rice from sticking to your hands). Dip in sesame seeds, place on serving dish and repeat until all rice has been formed into balls. If necessary, cover with plastic wrap and reheat in microwave for a minute before serving.

SAFFRON RISOTTO (202)

The classic accompaniment to Osso Buco, this rice dish is rich, creamy and addictive. For an extra decadent touch, add a little square of gold leaf on top when you serve. The creamy texture of risotto comes from using Italian medium-grain rice, which is starchier than regular rice. My favorite is Carnaroli but Arborio works well too. Hannibal only uses Vialone Nano but it is not widely available outside the Veneto region of Italy.

INGREDIENTS:

1 Tbsp butter
¼ onion, finely chopped
1 cup Carnaroli or Arborio rice
¼ tsp saffron threads, measured loosely
½ cup white wine
3 - 3½ cups chicken stock
1 Tbsp butter
¼ cup freshly grated Parmesan cheese
1 square gold leaf, optional

Yields **4** side servings,

1. In a heavy pot, heat olive oil over medium heat. Add onions and cook until translucent. Add rice and cook until rice turns a bit white and glassy, about 1 minute. Add saffron, wine and half of stock and bring to boil. Reduce heat and simmer, stirring constantly, until most of the liquid has been absorbed. Add another cup of stock and cook, stirring constantly until liquid has been absorbed. Continue cooking and adding stock until rice is soft but still a bit "al dente", about 20 minutes.

2. At this point, you can set the rice aside in a cool place for up to an hour and finish cooking it when it's almost serving time because the risotto must be served as soon as it is ready. Fifteen minutes before serving time, return the risotto to the heat and gradually add another ¼ cup of stock, stirring very gently to loosen the rice but not break the kernels. When it starts bubbling, add another ¼ cup of stock, stir for a few minutes to heat through, add butter and Parmesan, stir just to combine and ladle onto plate. It should not lump together nor be soupy but should flow a bit in its own juice when you spoon it out. Garnish with gold leaf. Serve immediately.

Curry Chicken and Butterfly Pasta Salad (111)

As we were shooting *Rôti*, there was much debate on what Hannibal would serve Dr Chilton. It had to be mutton because of the sheep references in the script and Bryan Fuller wanted to use intestines. I'm a big fan of South Asian food, so I suggested Aatu Kudal Kulambu, a south-Indian curry of sheep gut, served on sculpted banana leaves.

Guessing neither of the actors wanted to chew on entrails for pages and pages of dialogue, I made a lightly curried pasta for the scene using radiatori and rustic maccheroni coloured and shredded to look like sheep intestines.

This curried pasta salad is much like the preparation I made to stand in for Kudal. With the butterfly shaped pasta and the almonds and grapes on top – and minus the sheep entrails – it is easier to make and can be served in banana leaf bowls (p226). You can use a barbecued chicken from the deli to simplify the preparation and if Champagne grapes are not in season, use halved green or red grapes such as the Muscat variety.

INGREDIENTS:

½ cup mayonnaise
2 tsp Japanese curry powder or other
  mild blend

¼ cup toasted slivered almonds
¼ tsp ground cinnamon
¼ tsp icing sugar (powdered sugar)

1½ cup cooked farfalle pasta
1 cup shredded roast chicken
½ cup celery, cut in ¼" dice
¾ cup Champagne grapes, stems
  removed
salt, to taste

Yields **2-3** servings

1. In a small bowl, combine mayonnaise and curry powder. Set aside. In another small bowl, combine almonds, icing sugar and cinnamon. Set aside.

2. In a medium-sized mixing bowl, combine chicken, pasta, celery and half of the grapes. Toss together, add mayonnaise mixture and fold together until all ingredients are well-coated. Season with salt to taste. Turn out into serving platter or individual bowls made from banana leaves, sprinkle almonds on top, then the rest of the grapes.

SEA URCHIN

The first food scene for the Season 2 premiere was to be a close-up of Hannibal pulling a quivering orange lobe of sea urchin out of its spiny shell. It needed to have all the sensorial vividity that I could deliver – to satiate the viewers hungry for Hannibal after a long hiatus.

In full compliance with Murphy's Law, fresh sea urchins were out of season when we shot the scene. I had phoned up and down both coasts of the Americas and could not find any live urchins for sale. Luckily, my niece lives near the ocean in the Pacific Northwest. She agreed to go down to the docks and find a private diver willing to go out and bring up a dozen. Fantastic! Except that it would take 3 days to ship them to me because of the long holiday weekend. Sea urchins die in 3 days; they go brown and their spines fall off. Not a good visual.

Google had informed me that nothing will prevent the spines from dropping. But I had a plan: get the live sea urchins; clean them out completely; bury the shells in salt the way a taxidermist makes fish trophies; courier the dried shells to Toronto; refill them with lobes of fresh roe flown in from Chile. Ta dah!

Amazingly, it all went well. I had to glue back a few spines that had dropped and paint the shells red because they had gone a very sick shade of blech. But they smelled sweet as a sea breeze and looked gorgeous. A few weeks after the shoot, the local fish markets were awash in fresh sea urchins. The tyranny of the shooting schedule!

LINGUINI WITH SEA URCHIN CREAM (201)

Hannibal prepares sea urchin (*uni* on a sushi menu) as part of the kaiseki dinner he makes for Jack. It is an elegant sashimi to compliment the flounder Hannibal presents on a tempura fish skeleton. Uni has a squishy texture and the flavour is a bit unusual – similar to lobster tomalley or shrimp heads. For someone newly learning to love uni, here is a pasta dish enjoyed by another fictional gourmet, Italian Noir detective Montelbano, whose appetite is not as dangerous as Hannibal's.

INGREDIENTS:

5 oz linguini
2 Tbsp butter
6 slices fresh ginger
½ cup white wine
6 Tbsp whipping cream
3 oz fresh sea urchin roe (uni)

Yields **4** first course servings

1. In a large saucepan, add linguini to boiling water and cook according to directions. Drain, reserving about ¼ cup of water and return pasta to saucepan. Add 1 Tbsp butter, tossing until well-coated. Set aside.

2. In a heavy-bottomed saucepan over medium-high heat, add ginger and butter and cook until ginger browns. Remove ginger and discard. Add wine to saucepan and boil until reduced by half. Add cream and boil until slightly thickened. Add sea urchin and mash with a fork or purée with immersion blender until sea urchin has broken down and sauce is fairly smooth. Add salt to taste and add a bit of pasta water if sauce has thickened too much. Transfer pasta to the pot of sea urchin sauce and toss until well-coated. Transfer to four individual pasta bowls and serve.

Pappardelle sulla Lepre (305)

In *Contorno*, Inspector Pazzi and his young wife, Allegra, share a tenderly home-cooked dinner with Jack and discuss honour, marriage, and values. This meal, like all meals in *Hannibal*, is a time of truce – a momentary pause in killing and maiming to reflect and savour the moments that pass too quickly in these tragic, changing lives.

The original Etruscan recipe called for hare's blood to thicken and enrich the sauce – like the famous French dish Lièvre à la royale. The speedy, elusive hare captured and cooked in its own blood seems a most appropriate dish for the doomed Inspector Pazzi. In this recipe, tomatoes and flour take the place of blood.

Ingredients:

one 2½ lb rabbit
1 lg carrot, diced
1 onion, diced
2 ribs celery, diced
¼ tsp dried rosemary
¼ tsp dried thyme
2 tomatoes, diced
2 cups red wine
3 Tbsp olive oil
flour for dredging

1 lb fresh pappardelle*
1 Tbsp butter
salt and pepper to taste
shaved Parmesan cheese

Pappardelle is pasta shaped like fettuccini, but wider. You can buy it fresh or dried, or use fresh lasagna sheets roughly cut into strips 1" wide.

Yields **4** servings as first course, **2** as main course

1. Combine wine, carrots, onions, celery, rosemary and thyme in a large bowl. Cut rabbit into pieces and add to bowl. Marinate overnight. Drain and reserve liquid, meat, and vegetables separately. Pat rabbit pieces dry, dredge with flour.

2. Heat oil in large casserole pan, add diced vegetables, drained of marinade, and fry lightly. Add rabbit to casserole pan and brown. Add liquid from marinade, bring to boil and scrape bottom of pan to release all browned bits. Cover, reduce heat and simmer for 3 to 4 hours or until tender. Check occasionally, adding wine if necessary – there should be at least 1 cup of sauce in the casserole pan.

3. Take meat out of sauce, remove and discard bones, cut the meat into small pieces and put back into the casserole pan. The meat of the slow-cooked haunches is easily removed from the bone so can be served whole on the side.

4. When ready to serve add pappardelle to pot of boiling salted water and cook until al dente. Drain, toss with butter and Parmesan cheese.

5. Mound pappardelle in centre of large platter. Pour hare and sauce over the pappardelle and serve.

HAVING FRIENDS
FOR DINNER

DESSERTS
AND DRINKS

SUMMER PUDDING

Hannibal served a Norton grape jelly mould to Dr Chilton - made from the boiled bones and cartilage of some unfortunate soul but the recipe I'm giving you is for blood-red Summer Pudding. It is also a moulded fruit dessert but much more delicious and utterly fool proof – no people-bones required. This was the dessert I was planning for this scene until a last-minute script revision sent me scrambling on a 48-hr search scouring the globe for the Dreaded Norton Grape.

INGREDIENTS:

1 pt raspberries, washed
½ pt blueberries, washed
1 pt strawberries, washed, hulled and
    quartered
½ cup sugar
2-3 Tbsp Cointreau, optional
9-12 slices white sandwich bread, crusts
    removed

Yields **4** desserts

1. In a large saucepan over low heat, combine berries and sugar and allow to heat slowly, just until sugar melts completely. Remove from heat. Stir in Cointreau.

2. Line four 1-cup moulds or bowls with plastic wrap. Line the bottom and sides of the moulds with slices of bread, keeping 2-3 slices for the tops.

3. Spoon an equal amount of berries into each mould. Pour berry liquid over, also divided equally. Cover berries with reserved bread slices and pull plastic wrap up and over the tops, sealing as well as possible. Place in refrigerator with a small weight, such as a can of soup, on each pudding and allow to macerate overnight.

4. Unmould onto serving plates, remove plastic wrap and pour juice over spots of bread that have not been soaked through. Serve with whipped cream and decorate with sugared rose petals and buds (below).

SUGARED ROSE PETALS AND BUDS

INGREDIENTS:

1 egg white
1 cup sugar
3-6 fresh pesticide-free roses

1. In a small bowl, whisk egg white until frothy. If necessary, add a teaspoon of water to lessen the viscosity of the white. Pour some of the sugar into a pie pan or soup plate.

2. Remove outer petals of roses until there is just a tight bud on each stem. With a soft artist's brush, paint a petal on both sides with egg white. Transfer petal to the pan of sugar and using a soupspoon, sprinkle sugar evenly over the petal, coating it on both sides. Use a small dry paintbrush to knock off any large lumps of sugar that may collect. Transfer to a cake rack to dry. Repeat with remaining petals and coat buds with sugar in the same way. Set in a cool place to dry. When sugar has hardened they are ready to use as edible decoration.

After his dinner of Lambs' Tongues, Hannibal dares Dr Chilton to show his true colours, using Norton grapes as a metaphor, saying that they are admirable for having purple skins outside and purple flesh inside. A grape with nothing to hide.

This of course is not true but no one told me and I spent days searching world-wide for the mystical tone-on-tone Norton grape – always just out of reach. I finally found the North American authority on Norton grapes, Dr Colova, in her Florida University research lab. She gently assured me that ALL grapes are pale green inside and Nortons were no different. But a script is, well – scripture, so I had to supply grapes with purple flesh.

With 14 hours to go before everything was due on set, I raced out to the corner store and bought up all the grapes. I peeled them, dyed the flesh purple with food colouring and dipped them one by one in molten purple beeswax to give them back their inky skins, then fell asleep with my entire kitchen garlanded in tiny purple balls. After 4 hours of sleep, I got up, wound them together in clusters, gave them a dusting of rice flour for that fresh-off-the-vine look and dashed off to the studio. All so Hannibal could peel Chilton a grape.

CHEESE PLATTERS

While setting up the shot for the Norton grape scene, I piled a tray high with a splendid assortment of cheese, fruit and nuts and placed it in Hannibal's kitchen to add colour and texture to the background.

Cheese and fruit always make a beautiful addition to your table as a light bite or an after dinner savoury. Here are a few of my favorite seasonal combos.

SPRING:

Torta cheese (mascarpone layered gorgonzola) candied walnuts, Muscat grapes

SUMMER:

Tomato slices, fresh basil, sliced burrata cheese and French olives, crusty baguette

FALL:

Truffle Gouda cheese, black bread, Honeycrisp apples, roasted almonds

WINTER:

Bosc Pears, Vacherin Mont D'or cheese, dried figs and honey dates, roasted chestnuts

POMEGRANATE CHÈVRE (101)

Y ou can substitute grated aged cheddar for the Parmesan and add a splash of chili oil if you want a zippier flavour. Serve with crackers or with pita bread brushed with olive oil, cut into wedges, and toasted under the broiler.

If you want to make individual cheese plates for the last course of a sit-down dinner, make the recipe into 4 small balls, coating each one with pomegranate arils and serve each on a plate surrounded by crackers, nuts, grapes and fresh figs.

INGREDIENTS:

½ cup fresh chèvre, softened

¼ cup cream cheese, softened

½ cup grated Parmesan Reggiano or
   aged Asiago

¼ cup chopped walnuts

¼ cup chopped sun-dried tomatoes

1 tsp white wine, optional

1 tsp dried fines herbes*

1 cup pomegranate seeds (arils)

*substitute your favourite dried herbs or
1Tbsp of chopped fresh herbs*

Yields one **3"** cheese ball
or four 1½" balls

1. In a mixing bowl, using a fork, mash together cream cheese, chèvre, Parmesan and wine. Stir in walnuts, sun-dried tomatoes and fines herbes until well-blended. Refrigerate for at least 1 hour.

2. Shape cold cheese mixture into a ball and roll in pomegranate seeds until completely coated. Wrap with plastic wrap and refrigerate until ready to serve. Remove from fridge an hour before serving to let the cheese soften and the flavours develop.

POMEGRANATES

The very first time we see Hannibal's table, the camera lingers on a pomegranate. This was a fruit that quintessentialized our anti-hero. In Greek mythology, the pomegranate is beautiful and tempting but full of the seeds of retribution. Hades used this fruit to tempt Zeus' daughter. Before she could be rescued, she ate six seeds (called arils) so, forever hence, Dad had to allow her to stay with Hades in the underworld for as many months every year – thus cursing us annually with the barren spell of winter.

I used dozens of pomegranates over the seasons to garnish Hannibal's food, piling them high in Florentine bowls or tearing them open and scattering the seeds like ruby cabouchons onto Hannibal's glistening white plates: drops of blood on fresh snow.

In reality, pomegranates can be a bit difficult to serve – hard for diners to eat whole and impossible to spear the individual seeds. Here's a lovely presentation that has all the gorgeousness of pomegranates but none of the messiness.

INDIVIDUAL BREAD PUDDINGS WITH FRUIT

For the kitchen scene in *Fromage* (season 1, episode 8), I baked deep bread pudding in a large pans then cut the individual servings out using a 3" biscuit cutter. But this wastes a lot of yummy pudding, so I've adapted the recipe here to be made in large muffin tins.

I went through over 30 individual bread puddings when we shot this scene. It was two pages of dialogue between Will and Hannibal and the garnishing of the bread pudding was non-stop. Dolloping whipped cream, pouring sauce, sprinkling chocolate, positioning fruit… over and over and over. Until the unspeakable happened. I ran out of puddings.

When you are food styling for a scene, running out of food for resets is the nightmare of all nightmares. Cameras were rolling so I did the only thing I could. Luckily, it wasn't an eating scene so there weren't any food safety concerns. I reclaimed a dozen that had already been shot and sent to the dish pit. I rinsed them off, dusted them with brown sugar, zapped them with the butane torch and sent them out again. Hardest working puddings in Hollywood!

INGREDIENTS:

4 cups Italian bread, in 1" cubes, crusts removed
½ cup currants
2 cup milk
2 eggs
¼ cup sugar
1 tsp vanilla
2 Tbsp brown sugar
½ tsp cinnamon
1 tsp butter, softened

Yields **8** individual puddings

1. On a baking sheet, dry out the bread cubes in a 250°F oven until lightly browned. Using about ⅛ tsp butter per cup, coat inside of 8 cups of a large muffin tin. In a small bowl, mix together brown sugar and cinnamon and set aide. Separate one of the eggs, transferring the white to a bowl. Beat egg white until soft peaks form and set aside.

2. Transfer the yolk to a mixing bowl, then add milk, sugar, vanilla and the other egg. Beat the mixture until well-blended then stir in bread pieces and currants and set aside to soak until bread pieces have softened, about 10 minutes. Drain liquid off soaked bread cubes and add this liquid to the beaten egg white, gently fold together and set aside. Into prepared muffin tin, spoon enough bread mixture to cover the bottoms. Sprinkle ¼ tsp brown sugar mix over and ladle egg white mixture into muffin tin, dividing equally among cups. Filling cups with remaining bread mixture, mounding it up in the middle of each. Sprinkle the remaining brown sugar mix on the tops.

3. In an oven preheated to 325°F, bake for 20-25 minutes or until a knife tip inserted into the middle of a cup comes out clean. Transfer to plates while still warm and serve with fresh fruits, whipped cream and chocolate shavings. Drizzle with raspberry coulis (p215). Decorate with Broken Glass sugar shards if desired (p217).

ANGEL WINGS (CHIACCHIERE)

In the script, Hannibal serves the Sanguinaccio with Savoiardi biscuits — Italian ladyfingers that are sold everywhere ever since tiramisu became a fixture on Italian dessert menus. Here is a recipe for Chiacchiere, a delicious traditional alternative you can make if your neighbourhood ladies have run out of fingers.

INGREDIENTS:

3 Tbsp butter, softened

4 Tbsp sugar

1 egg

2 Tbsp orange liqueur (such as Triple Sec)

¼ tsp vanilla

1¼ cup flour

oil for deep frying

icing sugar, cinnamon for dusting

Yields about **3** dozen small cookies

1. In a mixing bowl, beat together butter and sugar with whisk. Beat in egg and whisk together until well blended. Beat in liqueur and vanilla. Add flour and stir with fork until well combined. Turn out onto floured board and knead a few times until dough is smooth and soft but not sticky. Knead in a little more flour if dough is sticky. Set aside to rest for 20 minutes.

2. Using a rolling pin, roll out dough on lightly floured board until very thin, about the thickness of a quarter. Using a pastry cutter, cut dough into strips 1½" wide. Then cut strips into rectangles 3" long. Cut a 2" long slash down the middle, along the length, of each rectangle. Gently pull one end of the rectangle through the cut in the middle and back out to make a bow tie shape. Repeat with remaining rectangles.

3. Heat oil in a deep fryer or a deep heavy frying pan over medium-high heat. The oil should be at least 1½" deep. When oil reaches 300°F, drop twisted dough strips in oil, 6 or 8 at a time. Cook, flipping to brown all sides, until golden and puffy. Remove from oil with a skimmer and drain. Repeat with remaining strips. Sprinkle fried cookies with icing sugar and cinnamon and serve with Sanguinaccio.

SANGUINACCIO DOLCE
WITH BISCUITS (308)

Through all the years we worked on *Hannibal*, I worried about when he would go to jail. From Thomas Harris' *The Silence of the Lambs*, we know he must end there one day. I don't think there are many smart dinner parties given in jail, so the day he is incarcerated, so ends my job.

Years and episodes passed. Then suddenly one day, I read it. On the last page of the *Digestivo* script: Hannibal surrenders to Jack and slides his glance to Will.

"I want you to know exactly where I am. And where you can find me."

The rest of the crew was conciliatory. "You will be back", they speculated. "There will be more food. He has to escape…or there's his Mind Palace. Surely he will have dinner parties there…"

Happily, there would be more cooking. Hannibal has been a model prisoner and Alana, now the head of BSCIA is letting him cook a treat for Dr Chilton, the foolhardy egomaniac, bestselling author of *Hannibal, the Cannibal*.

With a plastic spoon and portable burner, Hannibal once again performs elegant kitchen choreography to make this blood-tinged treat.

I presented the Sanguinaccio in hollowed out oranges with cinnamon sticks. This served two purposes: to look great within the simplicity required by the circumstance, and to avoid the use of china or glass, which Hannibal could have weaponized. Also, I felt the smell of the citrus and spice would be so appetizing it would allay any fear of eating blood. Nevertheless, for the shoot, I prepared a back-up batch of fake pudding in case Mads or Raul didn't want to eat Sanguinaccio, but the real thing was so intriguing, that everyone on set wanted to try it.

INGREDIENTS:

1 cup pork or beef blood
¾ cup milk
¼ cup cream
¾ cups sugar
7 oz bitter-sweet (85%) dark chocolate.
cinnamon, orange zest to taste
berries to garnish
whipped cream to top

Yields **6** servings

1. In the top of a bain-Marie or in a heat-resistant bowl resting over a pot of gently simmering water, combine blood, milk, cream and sugar. Over low heat, stir constantly until warm then stir in chocolate and continue cooking. Make sure the water in the pot below does not boil; it should barely simmer. You should be able to see a bit of steam faintly rising from the pudding in the pot above.

2. Cook, stirring constantly until mixture has thickened like a custard (about 20-30 minutes). Add dash of cinnamon if desired. Served warm or refrigerate for a firmer texture and serve with orange peel, fresh berries and cookies.

REBA'S CHERRY BERRY PIE

In a touching moment, Reba almost conquers the Red Dragon with a wedge of pastry. A girl can get almost anything she wants with a well-baked pie.

Ready-to-fill unbaked pastry pie shells can be purchased frozen and really simplify pie-making. If you thaw the pastry before baking, keep it cold in the refrigerator to get the flakiest result.

Because the season for fresh fruit is short, frozen cherries are great to use for pie but you must drain them well or your filling will be runny. The addition of blueberries rounds out the flavour and their pectin helps the filling set. Sour cherries make the best tasting pie, but can be harder to find than regular sweet cherries. If you use the sour ones, add more sugar to taste.

INGREDIENTS:

2 cups frozen cherries, thawed and drained
2 cups fresh blueberries
¾ cup brown sugar
¼ cup cornstarch
¼ tsp salt
¼ tsp cinnamon
½ tsp almond extract

one 9" unbaked pastry pie shell
5-6 stars cut from pastry for top.

Yields 1 9" pie

1. In a bowl, mix together brown sugar, cornstarch, salt and cinnamon. Set aside. In a medium-sized bowl, gently toss cherries with blueberries and almond extract then add the sugar mixture and toss well until all berries are well coated. Transfer to pie shell, place pastry stars on top of the filling. Refrigerate for 20 minutes before baking.

2. In an oven preheated to 400°F, bake on lowest rack for 20 minutes then reduce heat to 325°F and bake for an additional 35 minutes until pastry has browned. Cool for at least 3 hours before cutting.

OSSI DI MORTE

A few months into filming the first season, the international press had gathered at our studio one wintery day to hear about Martha De Laurentiis and Bryan Fuller's exciting new *Hannibal*. It seemed unkind to talk of food all morning then send them away hungry, so I made these cookies for them to munch on.

They look just like little dusty, white bones and are crunchy on the outside with a lacy hollow centre – like a marrow bone. A friend's mother had made them from an old Sicilian recipe and the minute I tried them I knew they were perfect for Hannibal.

Ossi di Morte means "Bones of the Dead" and are traditionally made for Day of the Dead celebrations. But every day is Day of the Dead to Hannibal, so bake away!

INGREDIENTS:

1¾ cups flour
2 cups icing sugar (powdered sugar)
2 tsp baking powder
½ tsp cinnamon
2 eggs
1 tsp vanilla
1 tsp almond extract

Yields about **3** dozen cookies

1. In a medium-sized mixing bowl, blend flour, sugar, baking powder and cinnamon.

2. In a second mixing bowl, beat egg with vanilla, then add to bowl of flour mixture and stir until well blended into a crumbly dough. Turn out onto a board and knead gently a few times until the dough forms a smooth ball. Roll dough into a long log about ½" in diameter. Cut log into 4" sticks.

3. To shape bones: With a paring knife, make a 1" lengthwise cut in the end of each 4" stick, splitting each end into a "Y". Fold each branch of the "Y"s over to form bulbous ends, mimicking the shape of a bone.

4. On a cookie sheet lined with parchment, place the bones about 1" apart. Let stand in a cool dry place, uncovered for at least 5 hours or refrigerated, uncovered overnight. This will allow a crust to form. In an oven preheated to 350°F, bake for 6-10 minutes or until cookies are brown around the tips. They will be very crunchy so if you like them softer, bake at 300°F. Bones of the Dead vary greatly from region to region; this is the Sicilian version and a bit of the chewy insides will ooze out of the cookies while baking so, while the cookies are still soft and warm from the oven, you can trim this off if you want your cookies to look more like bones.

Want protein in your beer? It's only human.

Beer is one of the oldest drinks made by man and it seems that brewers have always tested the limits with ingredients. Cock ale, made from boiled chickens was a health-giving restorative employed as early as the 17th century. You can almost picture Hannibal brewing vats of it in his private cellar when you read this home recipe printed in 1739 in *The Compleat Housewife:*

"Take ten gallons of ale, and a large cock, the older the better; parboil the cock, flay him, and stamp him in a stone mortar till his bones are broken (you must craw and gut him when you flay him); then put the cock into two quarts of sack, and put it to three pounds of raisins of the sun stoned, some blades of mace, and a few cloves; put all these into a canvas bag, and a little before you find the ale has done working, put the ale and bag together into a vessel; in a week or nine days time bottle it up; fill the bottle but just above the neck, and give the same time to ripen as other ale…"

In the 1920s, oyster beer was very popular. Brewers tossed a half-dozen oysters in the kettle while boiling the wort and they melted away by the end of the boiling process, leaving only hints of their gamey, metallic flavour. There is a current resurgence of oyster beer and some brewers are adding the shells as well with some going as far as using prairie oysters (yes, bull's testicles) to enhance the flavour.

Currently, meat beer is back in favour as the new hip hop. Adventurous craft brewers are getting attention and awards for meaty ales such as pig beer and goat brain beer while fans of bacon beer are enjoying their smoke and drinking it too. Recently one top chef in an offal mood added hearts and livers to his beer. Another well-known craft brewer in Wellington made headlines with Stag Semen beer which they touted as extra creamy and hand-pulled. They also made liver and chianti beer, so there's no doubt of the source of their inspiration.

MIRIUM BEERIUM (107)

In *Sorbet*, Alana drinks her first glass of Hannibeer, and sets off a controversy that rages still: if and how was beer brewed from people? Hannibal tells Alana that he made it especially for her and reveals that it has been aged two years in an oak Cabernet Sauvignon barrel – then steers the conversation to Mirium Lass, Jack's assistant. She has been missing for two years. Her disembodied arm has just surfaced… and it smells a bit oaky.

During the Hannibal hiatus, my assistant, Victoria Walsh, was working on her own book, *Canadian Cocktails*, but she took time out to create this cocktail for Alana. She combined concepts of wine and beer and layered in story lines from Hannibal and Italy – so there is vermouth for the wine barrel that housed Mirium's arm, Amaro for Italy and the bitterness to come, and lager for the heady lightness of unknowing.

INGREDIENTS:

1½ oz sweet vermouth, such as Carpano Antica Formula
¾ oz Amaro, such as Sibilla, Nonino, Averna or Meletti
½ oz freshly squeezed grapefruit juice
6 oz light lager, preferably Peroni
¼ grapefruit wheel

Yields **1** cocktail

1. Fill a Collins glass with ice. Pour in Carpano, Amaro and grapefruit juice. Top with beer. Stir to mix. Garnish with grapefruit.

SPARKLING SANGRIA

Once in a very long while, Hannibal might have a bottle of plonk in the house. Some rude guest might have brought over a lesser bottle that Hannibal would never serve. But sitting outside, tending the fire beneath his Paella Aire Libre, he might just grab a few oranges from an overhanging bough and squeeze them into a rough wine just for fun. Like this white sparkling sangria to drink with your seafood paella.

INGREDIENTS:

1 bottle of sparkling white such as Café de Paris
2 cups fresh fruit such as diced peaches, sliced strawberries, raspberries, blueberries
6 oz St Germain or citrusy liqueur

1. In a mixing bowl, combine fruit and liqueur and allow to macerate refrigerated for at least 4 hours. When ready to serve, fill glasses ¼ full of fruit, then pour over chilled sparkling wine until each glass is ¾ full. Serve.

Yields **6** drinks

THE CHESAPEAKE RIPPER

John Krusii, my super-shopper and assistant was also our mixologist. He designed this sophisticated cocktail for my first *Hannibal* Pop-up Dinner.

INGREDIENTS:

2 ounces shiitake-infused scotch (recipe below)
½ ounce Gonzalez Byass Nectar Pedro Ximénez Dulce Sherry
3 dashes Fee Brother's Black Walnut Bitters
2 dashes Regan's Orange Bitters No. 6
scotch-infused cherries (recipe below)
fresh thyme sprig, optional

1. In a cocktail shaker filled with ice add the scotch, sherry, and both bitters. Stir to mix and strain into a small tumbler over ice. Garnish with cherries, skewered on sprig of thyme if desired.

Yields **1** cocktail

SHIITAKE-INFUSED SCOTCH

These proportions can be easily multiplied for larger batches. John used Compass Box Great King Street Artist's Blend Scotch because it plays well with other ingredients and is less expensive than a single malt.

INGREDIENTS:

2 Tbsp dried shiitake mushrooms
8 oz blended scotch

1. In a clean jar add mushrooms and pour over scotch. Cover and leave to infuse for 1 hour. Strain mushrooms through a fine-mesh sieve or cheesecloth, to ensure all mushroom particles are removed.

SCOTCH-INFUSED CHERRIES

This also works well with other spirits such as bourbon or rye.

INGREDIENTS:

¼ cup granulated sugar
2 oz cold water
A few sprigs of lemon-thyme or regular thyme
4 oz scotch
½ cup good quality dried cherries

1. Combine the sugar, water and thyme in a small pot and bring to a boil. Remove from the heat and add the scotch and cherries. Cover cherries and leave to plump for approximately 30 minutes. Transfer to a resealable jar and refrigerate, covered, until ready to use.

PUNCH ROMAINE (303)

This is the cocktail served during the knock-out round for Sogliato where Hannibal proves to Bedelia that a couple can choose friends independently, but it's better if you pick your enemy together.

Orange peel garnish can be easily made by pulling strips of peel from the orange using a potato peeler, or use a canele cutter– a special tool that pulls thin strips of peel.

INGREDIENTS:

1 egg white
2 oz white rum
2 oz white wine
1 oz simple syrup
2 oz lemon juice
2 oz orange juice
4 oz Champagne or sparkling white
   wine
orange peel twists

Yields **2** drinks

1. In a cocktail shaker, combine 1 cup ice with egg white, rum, simple syrup, lemon, and orange juice. Cover and shake vigorously until frothy and cold. Mound crushed ice in two chilled coupe-style glasses and strain half of the contents of the shaker into each coupe. Top each with Champagne. Garnish with orange peels and serve.

ACHIEVING THE HANNIBAL LOOK

CHAPTER ONE

THE FOOD STYLIST'S LOCKER

1. TRICKS, TIPS AND TRAUMAS OF THE TRADE

Cooking for *Hannibal* engaged each and every skill I had acquired in my checkered career as an advertising art director, caterer, florist, author, couturier, painter and sculptor. Yet it was unlike anything I had ever done before.

Each episode began like any other film job I had previously done: read the script, make a plan, do it, cash the cheque. But *Hannibal* was different. A whirlwind of unintended incidents spun out from every page of every script: searching outlying abattoirs for extra-large bung and extra-small hearts; accidentally exploding lungs in a borrowed industrial-strength vacuum-packager; enduring the miasma in my car of evaporating dry ice that kept summer's heat from damaging my ill-gotten veal brains; the constant drip of blood oozing from my fridge… this is no job for a lady.

But three seasons later, I want you to consider me your culinary courier de bois who boldly cut through new territory so you could bring Hannibal's gore and glory to your own dinner table – sans people-ingredients of course.

Even the Menu is Good Enough to Eat!

Richard Armitage gets hungry just looking at his Blake's Red Dragon etching. So we had to make credible edible copies for his etching-eating scenes.

You can do the same for menus for your *Hannibal* dinner party! Rice paper and edible ink felt-tip markers can be ordered from cake-decorating supply stores and you can hand-letter each menu. Or you can email your art to an edible print-maker (no, no - the prints are edible, not the maker) who can duplicate your menus on rice paper or candy sheets using food-grade inks in their ink-jet copier.

Out Out, Damn Spot!

Bloodwork, fake: Needless to say, we went through mega-gallons of blood while shooting all those murders and mirages. Fake blood, of course. Every department had their own custom-made blood. Mine often had to be both beautiful and delicious so was made from crushed seeded raspberries. On less epicurean days, it was simply corn syrup and red food colouring.

Bloodwork, real: Finding real blood to cook with can be problematic and I got mine straight from a local abattoir who exported most of theirs to cigarette manufacturers. (It is used in some filters to trap harmful chemicals released in smoking tobacco.) Blood, although full of nutrition and widely available is rarely sold for human consumption, so you may have to search a bit to find a supplier. Some butchers in Chinese supermarkets carry fresh raw blood, or try South American butchers who use it to make blood sausage.

Modelling Clay You Can Eat.

Edible noses: If Michael Pitt has to cut off his nose and eat it, he'll need fake nose skin. The best material is to use is marzipan. It can be coloured and shaped into just about anything and I used it to make fake snails, weird mushrooms and, most memorably, dozens of tiny ortolans for Season 2's *Ko No Mono*. When you buy marzipan make sure it's soft and malleable. Some varieties are quite hard and difficult to work with. Colour the marzipan with food colouring and after you model it into the shape you want, let it air-dry and harden for a day or two. Marzipan ears, anyone?

Edible bones: While I was on *Hannibal* hiatus, I sneaked over to the sound stage down the street where *Hemlock Grove* was being shot. That's what a cannibal cook does on holiday: she cooks for TV vampires.

The *Hemlock* scene called for the vampire-princeling to rip the bone out of a lamb shank, crack it in half and suck out the bloody marrow. So I made breakable shank bones out of Baker's Clay and filled them with red jelly. Baker's Clay is made by mixing 4 parts flour with 1 part salt and stirring in 1.5 parts water and kneading until smooth. Then you sculpt it into the desired shapes and bake at 300°F until it's completely dry. This is a great toxin-free clay to work with and the baked pieces last forever. I used it to fake up venison roasts on a film where the director was vegan and no meat was allowed on set.

There Must be a Zoo Somewhere That's Just Lost a Giraffe...

Impossible requests: Ever stop yourself in the middle of something and realize "one more step and you'd have gone too far"? I have faked people-parts out of various cuts of pork, goat, lamb and veal. In close-up shots, they stood in beautifully for human cuts.

But one day I was asked for a whole leg that Hannibal could carve like a butcher... the full hip to knee to ankle of bones and muscles to lay bare before the camera. No, I replied, even while knowing that was not an acceptable answer. Thinking I might be able to get a leg of horse or camel from my suppliers of exotic meats, I phoned around. Yes, those meats were available but not in one whole piece on the bone.

Deep in search-mode, I started to look up zoos thinking maybe a giraffe died that week. That could work. Then I stopped myself. Because, no.

I went back to the director and told him there was no way I could get a real leg the size of a man's. Sometimes No means NO.

Was it Fantasy or the Reel Thing?

Prosthetics: Every day at work, there were fake dead people on dollies, trolleys and just lying about, in part or in whole or just hanging from the ceiling. From the plotlines, these were destined to be ingredients in Hannibal's dishes. In the filming, there was always a point where fake bodies became real meat and this is where the magic lies. Much of the fun of feeding Hannibal came from collaboration with make-up and prosthetics crews. Would I stitch fake skin on a real pork shank or would I manipulate the pork skin to look like human skin? Can I make a real heart "beat" or should we put a balloon pump inside a prosthetic heart? Would you like fries with that ear?

Livestock and their wranglers: On set we had real animals from trout and tiny maggots to all the creatures of the farmyard. Like movie stars, all were accompanied by their squad – each group of animal having their own set of trainer/wranglers minding the animals' hours, working conditions and their feed. Snail wrangler: that's a real job. Food for thought.

Green screen: is used when the action is shot in one location but the background of a different place will be edited in later. Like the background of Hannibal and Will's fight and fall in the final episode. Their scene, filmed up-country in Ontario was greenscreened into a wind-strafed cliff near an abandoned mine in Belle Isle, Newfoundland. Beautifully shot by Chris Burne's crew hanging out of a helicopter as it buzzed the shore, scattering a few night birds that were circling — or was that just Hannibal and Will transforming again?

As the food stylist, I was not required on set every day. Once every week or two I would show up at the sound stage, set up my station, get my food prepped, then wait for my scene. Sometimes I would wait for hours. What to do? Stroll through the darkened sound stage to check out the other sets, get snacks from craft service, go to the washroom, visit the makeup trailer to warm up. There were always amazing things on the *Hannibal* sound stage. Sometimes a taxidermied horse flopped out on its side by the washrooms (guess it didn't really want to go), or a life-like tiger "puppet" motorized to "breathe" and bodies in various stages of scorched or slashed that were unbearably realistic. It was a three-ring circus of astonishment where extraordinarily gifted artisans plied their arts. And I, the food juggler, just one of the many passing behind the lights.

II. Inside the Mind of Hannibal:

E at the Rude: I don't usually take script directions from t-shirts, but when I first got the job and began acquainting myself with Hannibal, I saw this saying emblazoned on everything: Eat the Rude. That phrase gave me all the insight I needed to cook like Hannibal. As Claude Levy-Strauss pointed out in *The Raw and the Cooked*, civilization is defined by the degree to which it applies technique to raw material to make it refined. With the cool hand of a surgeon, Hannibal slashes, chops, binds and grinds the rude into dishes of haute cuisine. Relentlessly making them better.

Inspired by Art: The vain excess depicted in 17ᵗʰ century Flemish still-life paintings was a direct inspiration for me in creating the look of Hannibal's food. The voluptuous overblown flowers, partially eaten roasts and decadent rotting fruit displayed on lush brocades had the baroque inner life I thought personified Hannibal — a complex creature of mannered excess steeped in another age, yet living in comfortable contrast to his sleekly elegant sets. Salvador Dali's art had a great influence on me too, full of lustful food symbology, insect-ridden carcasses and beheaded saints crawling with crayfish. Always executed with wicked humour.

Steered by the script: Everything and everyone in Bryan Fuller's scripts seemed to be on a knife-edge, so I wanted the food to be dangerously balanced, too, and to occupy the liminal space between tempting and lethal, good and evil, dead and alive. Food is one of those things that can kill you. We show a great deal of trust in the cook when we eat his food, but there is always an element of danger: it can soothe like mother's milk or kill like polonium tea.

Dinner conversation with Hannibal: Food is a metaphor. Hannibal is always reminding his guests of this in a manner that Fannibals have described as "How to speak like Hannibal". For example, in this conversation with Will:

1 Make a wordy overblown remark about an element of the dinner.

2 Refer this back to your guest by adding "tell me, Will, what…"

3 Finalize with a random phrase excerpted from (1).

Example: "The plastic tablecloth is a thin superstratial layer of hydrophobic material. In the event of liquid spillage or overflow, it protects the chatoyancy and grain of my priceless mahogany table.[1] Tell me Will,[2] what will protect your brain — I mean, grain?"[3]

ACHIEVING THE HANNIBAL LOOK

CHAPTER TWO

HOW TO HANNIBALIZE YOUR TABLE

1. Garnishes and Hannibalisms

Quoth the Ravenstag, Nevermind: Normally, I would never garnish a plate with anything inedible. But surrounded by stags and ravens, who could resist adding cock feathers and animal horns to Hannibal's plates. Still, it's best to keep these inedible garnishes to the side of your platters where they won't get dragged into the sauce. Cock feathers can be found at millinery supply shops. They come in iridescent black or bleached and dyed in many colours. Peacock and pheasant feathers are sold in craft shops and floral supply shops. Plastic insects can be purchased from science and toy shops.

Scary vegetables: Next time you are choosing produce or cutting through a bell pepper, look at it as if you are seeing it for the first time. You will see faces everywhere – and wherever there aren't faces, there will be snakes. It's just the way our reptilian brain works – always on the lookout for predators. A turnip can look like a skull and an anchovy becomes a wiggling worm. You don't have to be a sculptor to make your food look like it's watching you. Did you see the face in that toast? Jesus!

White vegetables look like skull and crossbones with very little trimming. Check out white asparagus, sliced fresh lotus roots and white baby carrots. Mushrooms look scary just because of their natural tendency to grow on deadwood.

Some fruits just look like aliens. Look in Asian supermarkets for Custard apples, Buddha's Hand, Dragonfruit, Rambutan, Finger limes. These tropical fruits are fascinating and delicious.

Did I mention blood?

Raspberry Coulis

Here is a blood-red sauce to Hannibalize your sweet presentations. Drizzled or pooled on your ice creams, puddings and pastries, it will look bloody good, taste delicious and never leave your DNA at the scene. For blood pooling on savoury dishes, add a few ingredients to make Cumberland Sauce (p123).

Ingredients:

12 oz bag frozen raspberries, thawed
sugar, to taste
2 Tbsp liqueur such as Framboise or
   Chambord, optional

Yields **1½** cups

1. With a large sieve positioned over a bowl, pour half of the raspberries and juices into sieve and press through mesh with the back of a large spoon. This will remove the seeds. Scrape the resulting purée off the outside of the sieve and into the bowl. Discard seeds. Repeat with the remaining berries.

2. Stir in sugar if necessary and liqueur if desired. Spoon purée onto dessert plate and arrange dessert on top, or drizzle over ice cream, fruit salad, pudding or pastry.

Tomato Blossom Skewers

These skewers can be used as attelettes to spear garnishes onto a steak or a roast chicken or as skewers for hors d'oeuvres. Great for swizzle sticks in cocktails like Bloody Marys.

1. Push a skewer into the stem end of a cherry tomato. Using a very sharp paring knife, score a shallow cut around the north-south axis of the tomato, not quite to the stem end. At 90° to the first line, score another cut around the tomato, intersecting the first line at the blossom end.

2. Hold the tomato in boiling water for about 1 minute, or until the peel starts to curl away from the blossom end of the tomato. Remove and run under cold water. Gently peel down the skin of the tomato, one section at a time until the 4 sections are fanning out around the tomato like a sepal. Using the paring knife tip, ease open the X-cut tomato flesh so it resembles a four-petal bud. The thin skin should peel away easily. If it doesn't, hold the tomato in boiling water for a longer period of time.

TOMATO ROSES

Hannibal deftly forms large roses out of tomatoes to dazzle his guests in *Sorbet*. You can make the same beautiful roses, but in many sizes and colours by using big beefsteak tomatoes, heirloom Roma tomatoes and cherry tomatoes.

1. Using a small, very sharp knife, starting at the blossom end, pare the peel off a tomato in one continuous strip and, working in a spiral around the tomato, finishing at the stem end. As you cut off the peel, include a thin layer of flesh. Shape the blossom end of the strip into the rose centre by rolling it, skin side out, into a tight bud. Wind the peel around the bud and a rose will naturally form. Nestle sprigs of fresh basil or plat leaf parsley next to the roses.

ONION CHRYSANTHEMUMS

Easy to make and always mysteriously beautiful, these can be made in various sizes depending on the onions you use. I loved using them for Hannibal whenever there was an octopus on the table – the curling purple tentacles made the onion flowers look like sea anemones. The best thing is, after they have done their work as garnishes, you can chop them up and use them later for stews and soups!

1. Using a red onion, peel papery brown outer skin away. Trim off root hairs as well as the papery ends from the top of the onion.

2. Place the root end in the ring part of a mason jar lid. This will steady the onion and also prevent you from cutting all the way through the onion. Starting at the centre of the top, slice onion through the middle, cutting down to within ½" of the root. Rotate onion 45° and slice down again, stopping ½" before the root. Repeat until onion is sliced in eighths. Slice each eighth into 3-4 sections until the whole onion has been cut into thin wedges about ⊠" wide. Make sure all wedges are connected at the root end. In a deep bowl or pail of ice-water, immerse and chill for at least 4 hours or overnight.

CANDY GLASS SHARDS AND ARTERIAL SPRAY

Easy and gorgeous, these special decorative touches add a dramatic touch to your food presentation. Just be careful with the molten sugar – it is very, very hot. Wear rubber gloves if you have to handle it while it is liquid and sticky.

MATERIALS:

2 cups sugar
½ cup white corn syrup
1 cup water
5-6 drops red food colouring (optional)

1. Prepare a pan by greasing lightly with butter or use a silicone baking sheet.

2. In a heavy saucepan, combine sugar, corn syrup and water. Boil over medium-high heat until 295°F (almost hard crack). Remove from heat, cool for a few minutes and gently stir in food colouring if desired. Red for arterial spray, of course.

3. Using a ladle with an insulated handle, pour syrup onto baking sheet in desired shape. Use rubber gloves or oven gloves for this operation. If syrup starts to harden while you are still working with it, return to medium-low heat to liquefy. Once the poured pieces cool enough to handle, they can be pulled, twisted or draped over a rolling pin into the shape you want. If you want to extend the working time, warm the poured pieces in an oven preheated to 250°F. Allow to harden and store in a cool dry place until ready to use.

CANDY APPLE AND PEAR GARNISH (301)

Poor Gideon. Hannibal eats him limb by limb. We are shocked in Season 2 when Hannibal feeds Gideon his own thigh baked in clay. Then, in Season 3, we see his other leg candied, skewered and served back to him on a bed of smoking thyme. Gideon, never without wry comment, smells the sweet spices and compares Hannibal to the cannibalistic Wicked Witch who lured Hansel and Gretel with her deliciously decorated gingerbread house.

I garnished Gideon's long pork leg with candied fruit to reinforce the dialogue about the wicked witch. You can garnish your smaller platter of pork belly with tiny Lady Apples and little Sugar Pears. I used a clear candy to give them the look of Venetian hand-blown glass but you can add yellow or red food colouring – even black if you want dramatic colours. Wear rubber gloves while making these – the syrup is dangerously hot.

MATERIALS:

3 Lady Apples
3 Sugar Pears
2 cups sugar
½ cup white corn syrup
1 cup water
5-6 drops food colouring (optional)
6 twigs or skewers

1. Skewer each apple and pear securely through stem end. Prepare a pan by greasing lightly with butter.

2. In a heavy saucepan, combine sugar, corn syrup and water. Boil over medium-high heat until 295°F (almost hard crack). Remove from heat, cool for a few minutes and gently stir in food colouring if desired.

3. Holding it by the skewer, carefully dip an apple, swirling gently to cover all sides, tilting the pot (carefully!) if necessary. Lift out of hot syrup and allow excess to drip off. Place upright on prepared pan. Repeat with remaining apples and pears. If syrup starts to harden, return to medium-low heat to liquefy. Allow dipped fruit to harden, remove skewers and store in a cool dry place until ready to serve.

BLOOD SPURTS FOR CANDIED APPLES

After dipping apples and pears in red coloured candy, you can make blood spurts from the remaining syrup. Line a baking sheet with parchment then, using a long-handled spoon, drop spoonfuls of hot syrup on the parchment forming elongated teardrop shapes. Allow to harden. Poke holes in candied fruit with an icepick or small knife and position the thin end of a candy shape into each hole so it looks like it's spurting out of the fruit.

BROKEN GLASS SHARDS

After dipping fruit, pour leftover hot syrup onto parchment-lined baking sheets and allow to flow out into thin sheets. When hardened and cooled, put sheets, one at a time, into a clean plastic bag and tap with the back of a spoon to break into shards. Remove and store in a cool dry place. These shards can be used to decorate cupcakes or puddings by stabbing the sharp ends into the tops at different angles.

FIERY RED DRAGON BABYBEL PLACE CARDS

Throughout the making of *Hannibal* and beyond, wonderful Fannibals showed their love through a prodigious volume of fanart, amazing in its quality and creativeness. When Red Dragon leaves a half-eaten Babybel cheese in his victim's fridge, some were inspired to make wax art that in turn inspired these edible place card holders.

MATERIALS:

For each place card:

2 Babybel cheeses in red wax for each place card
one ¾" x 3" ribbon or strip of paper inscribed with guest's name

1. Remove all wax and paper pull-strip from one of the cheeses and remove half of the wax and paper strip from the other. Reserve wax and paper strips and set aside. Using a small spoon, remove and discard a tooth-shaped "bite" from the cheese that is still half covered in wax. Set aside.

2. Make the dragon wings: Using wax shell from one cheese, flatten the two halves of wax to make 2 semi-circles. Using the tip of a very small spoon, notch these out on the curved side to resemble dragon wings. Set aside.

3. Make the candle: Scrape wax off paper strips and twist paper together tightly into a wick 1" long. Cut the remaining wax shell half into strips ¼" wide and along with other wax scraps, roll tightly around paper wick to make candle, leaving paper wick exposed on one end.

4. Press candle bottom onto the middle of the wax shell of "bitten" cheese. Press dragon wings behind candle. Place this on top of the other whole cheese and tuck the inscribed ribbon between the two. Keep refrigerated until ready to use. Just before guests are seated, put the cheese place card on a small plate at the place setting and light the candle.

II. The Art of the Dish

Bone Candlesticks and Bud Vases

B eef marrow bones are available at most butcher shops and often sold frozen in 4-5" lengths. Ask the butcher to cut some of them in half if you want shorter candleholders. Get whole bones, not canoe-cut, so they can be stood on end and used as holders for tall dinner candles and bud vases. For dramatic centrepieces, they can be clustered together in groupings of 3 and 5 and surrounded by white flowers, small animal skulls and a scattering of small bones that you can collect in the freezer when you have a roast.

Materials:

beef marrow bones in 3-6" lengths
hydrogen peroxide, 3% solution
Plasticine or other soft, non-drying
   modelling clay

1. Collect used bones in the freezer. When you have accrued enough to make an arrangement, put them in a large pot and cover with water. Heat over medium-high heat and boil gently for about 2-3 hours until all bits of meat, gristle and marrow have detached from the bones. Drain and rinse with cool water. Transfer bones into a large bowl or pail filled with warm soapy water and, using an old toothbrush, scrub bones completely clean. Drain and allow to dry.

2. Using a large soft artist's brush, paint bones liberally with peroxide and let them air-dry, preferably in sunlight. This will gently bleach the bones to a natural ivory colour.

3. Shape a 1" ball of Plasticine or plumber's mastic for each marrow bone and push a ball into one end of each marrow bone. Stand each bone on end, Plasticine end down, and press until ball flattens and marrow bone stands upright on its own. This will allow you to fill the bone with water for use as a bud vase and also keep the bone balanced if you use it as a candleholder.

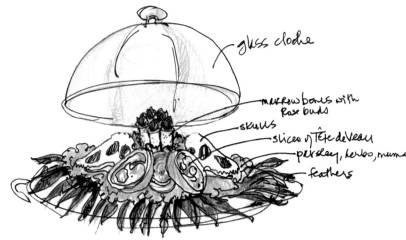

glass cloche

marrow bones with
Rose buds

skulls

slices of Tête de Veau

parsley, herbs, mums

feathers

SHELL GAMES

Nature loves to creep us out. Whether she's covering things in honeycomb or revealing decay, she reminds us of mortality with her wild artistry. She is especially demonic in her deep-sea creations. That's why I loved using seashells at Hannibal's table. While they make beautiful vessels there is always something other-worldly about them. Like Hannibal himself.

Nautilus: Bisected to display the inner chambers, they can be used as plates for balancing escargots or stuffed clams. The proportions of the chambers follow the Golden Mean, which is said to be the perfect ratio between opposites and, when applied geometrically, creates the most beautiful art and architecture. Used whole, nautilus can be filled with olives or crudité like a sea horn of plenty.

Giant barnacles: Several clusters of these shells can be used to prop up piles of oysters, mussels or shrimp. Their individual craters can be stuffed with tiny flowers or something scarier like smoked baby squid or shrimp heads.

Oversized scallop shell or abalone shells: The half-shells can be used as small dishes for caviar or sauces or salts.

Giant clam shells: These impressive half-shells can be used as bowls for pasta and rice salads, or filled with crushed ice and used as a fresh oyster platter. Surrounded with spring flowers, it's like a Botticelli on your buffet table!

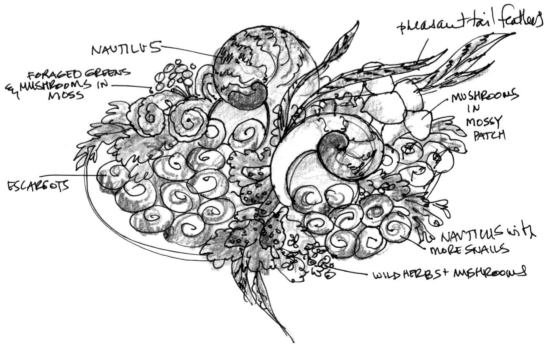

MIGNONETTE OYSTER DISH

W hen you serve oysters like Beach Angel or Marinas Top Drawer, it's hard to throw away the beautiful shells, dramatically ruffled on the outside and mother of pearl on the inside. Here's a simple dish you can make from them that will decorate the table as well a function as a sauce dish or candleholder.

MATERIALS:

10-15 oyster shells
1 small ceramic bowl
1 glass saucer

hot glue gun or non-drying modelling
    clay

1. Using a glue gun or modelling clay, secure the bowl to the centre of the plate.

2. Use the bottom shells of the oysters: their cupped shape resembles a flower petal more than the upper shells, which are flat. Holding cupped side toward the centre and hinge end toward the plate, use glue or modelling clay to secure the shells to the plate closely around the bowl like the petals of a flower. Secure more rows of shells around the first for larger fuller flower. Fill the bowl with sauce or drop a votive candle in it.

EN PAPILLOTE LOTUS CUPS

Hannibal served Lamb Tongues in these origami lotus cups folded from parchment. These cups can be made from larger parchment squares and used as individual bowls for many things like baked pasta, tempura, edamame or candied nuts.

You can use the same procedure to fold starched dinner napkins to look like a large lotus flower.

MATERIALS:

one 14" x 14" square parchment paper
for each cup

1. Fold up lotus: fold square on the diagonal both directions so you have an X scored from corner to corner. Open out flat and fold each corner into the middle of the X, scoring folds as you go. The square will now be 10" x 10". Now fold the four new corners into the middle, score folds to make a square 7" x 7". Fold new corners in again so the square of paper is 5"x 5". Turn over and fold the corners into the centre once.

2. Open the lotus: on the underside of the folded square, push your finger into the corner pocket made by one of the four flaps, and pressing with your thumb from above onto the corner, gently pull the flap and ease it up and over the corner to form a little cupped petal. Repeat on other three corners and on next layers beneath. By the time you have brought the last rows up, the first two rows will have formed into a lotus. Put this on the plate and place two Kibbeh Tongues in the middle. Garnish with Duxelles (see recipe in Silver Tongue Devils, p101) and sour cream or yoghurt.

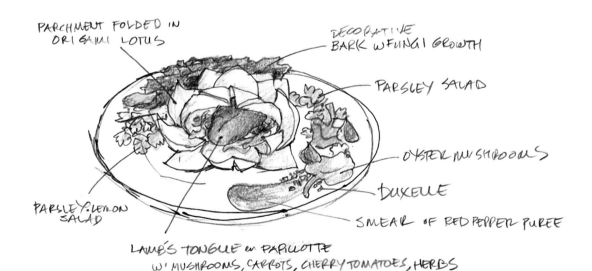

PARCHMENT FOLDED IN ORIGAMI LOTUS

DECORATIVE BARK w/FUNGI GROWTH

PARSLEY SALAD

OYSTER MUSHROOMS

DUXELLE

SMEAR OF RED PEPPER PUREE

PARSLEY-LEMON SALAD

LAMB'S TONGUE en PAPILLOTTE w' MUSHROOMS, CARROTS, CHERRY TOMATOES, HERBS

BANANA LEAF BOWLS

In *Roti*, Hannibal serves curried entrails in bowls made from banana leaves which he probably got by astral travelling to Mindanao. You can acquire them more easily in the freezer section of most Asian and Latin American grocery stores. Once thawed, they can be unfolded, rinsed well and used as cooking wraps for steamed or baked foods like Sri Lankan lumpries, Colombian pasteles, Mexican tamales, Malaysian lempur or use instead of lotus leaf to wrap your clay-baked thighs.

MATERIALS:

1 package frozen banana leaves (4-5 leaves)
toothpicks

1. Cut washed banana leaves into 8" circles. Layer 2 circles together and make a dart, 1" deep and 1" from perimeter. Staple dart together or use toothpick to secure. Repeat 3 times spaced equally around perimeter resulting in a 4-cornered bowl. Repeat with pairs of leaf circles until you have the number of bowls you want. If leaves are fresh, not frozen, blanch them in boiling water for a minute to make them flexible enough to fold easily.

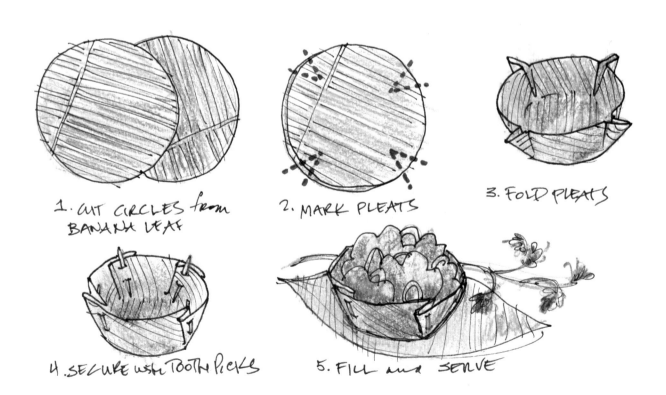

1. CUT CIRCLES from BANANA LEAF

2. MARK PLEATS

3. FOLD PLEATS

4. SECURE with TOOTH PICKS

5. FILL and SERVE

III. THERE'S A CENTREPIECE IN YOUR CRISPER

CAESAR'S GARDEN

A platter of Caesar Salad arranged to look like a philosopher's walk in a miniature brook-side garden.

MATERIALS:

I framed mirror about 10" x 15"
1 recipe Caesar Salad Bouquets (p 164)
1 bunch frisée

Parmesan Pumpernickel Dirt (p 230)

assorted sprouts
edible flowers

To assemble Garden:

1. Place 2 or 3 Caesar Salad Bouquets upright on the mirror and surround with assorted sprouts and edible flowers like a miniature garden. Use Pumpernickel Dirt to define reflecting pools or natural streams, leaving areas of the mirror visible to represent the water.

SHALLOW VEGGIE GRAVE

INGREDIENTS:

2 cup black quinoa, cooked
2-3 small basil plants
assorted sprigs of fresh herbs
cluster mushrooms such as Shemiji, Oyster, Hen-of-the-Woods
lotus roots, raw, peeled and sliced ¼" thick
baby vegetables such as coloured broccoli, pattypan squash, zucchini, carrots, French radishes
cherry tomatoes roses (p216)
cleaned empty marrow bones (p70)

Beet Vinaigrette (p170)

1. Remove basil plants from their flowerpots and gently shake off the dirt. Rinse all dirt off the roots and set plants aside.

2. On either a large oval platter, a washed and oiled wooden plank, or a clean marble slab, heap quinoa in the middle and stick in slices of lotus root to represent rising ghosts. Arrange root vegetables half-buried in quinoa. Surround with mushrooms, basil and tomato roses. Garnish with marrow bones. Sprinkle with Beet Vinaigrette.

PARMESAN PUMPERNICKEL DIRT

INGREDIENTS:

6 slices pumpernickel or dark rye bread
4 Tbsp butter
2 Tbsp grated Parmesan cheese

1. Cut crusts from bread and dry in oven at lowest temperature setting. When bread is completely dry and crispy, crush into breadcrumbs with a rolling pin.

2. Over medium heat, melt butter in sauté pan. When bubbling and just beginning to brown, add pumpernickel crumbs and toss quickly using a spatula so the breadcrumbs are evenly coated with butter. Sprinkle in Parmesan and stir over heat until breadcrumbs are toasted. Remove to a bowl and set aside to cool.

FLORENTINE FRUIT TRAY

INGREDIENTS:

1 cantaloupe
2 cups strawberries
2 cups large green grapes
½ cup marshmallow fluff
4 oz cream cheese, softened
toothpicks

Yields platter for **6-8** desserts

1. In a mixing bowl, beat cream cheese with a fork or a beater until smooth. Add marshmallow fluff and stir together until blended. Keep at room temperature until ready to serve.

2. Using a green felt-tip pen, lightly draw a pattern of fleur-de-lis and swirls all over the cantaloupe, then carve these lines out using a caneler, a V-groove whittling tool or the point of a paring knife. Carve just deep enough to cut through the beige peel and reveal the layers of green and orange. Slice off the bottom third of cantaloupe, remove and discard the seeds. Using a melon baller, scoop out flesh of cantaloupe in balls, and setting balls aside in a bowl. Using a tablespoon, scoop out the rest of the flesh from both pieces of melon to make the inside surface smooth.

3. Fill the smaller cantaloupe piece with marshmallow cream. Fill the larger cantaloupe with melon balls, grapes and strawberries, spilling some over on the tray to keep the cantaloupe pieces from tipping over. Stick toothpicks in the melon balls and grapes to facilitate dipping.

230

GINGER COOKIE DOUGH

This recipe will yield more dough than you need to make an Eye of God Bowl (p232), so roll, cut out and bake the rest for cookies to put into the finished bowl, or freeze the dough for another time.

INGREDIENTS:

½ cup butter, softened at room
    temperature
½ cup brown sugar
⅔ cup molasses
1 egg
3½ cups flour
1 tsp baking soda
2 tsp ginger
1 tsp cinnamon

1. In a large mixing bowl, stir butter and sugar together with a fork. Stir in molasses and egg. Beat well.

2. In another bowl, sift flour, baking soda, and spices together and add to butter mixture. Stir until well combined. Turn out onto counter and knead a few times until dough is smooth and soft. Add flour if sticky. Cover with plastic wrap and refrigerate at least 1 hr.

3. Using rolling pin on lightly floured surface, roll dough to ¹⁄₁₆" thickness, cut into desired shapes, arrange on baking sheets with 1" around each cookie, and bake in an oven preheated to 350°F for 10-12 minutes until edges begin to brown.

Yields **4** dozen cookies

VANILLA COOKIE DOUGH

INGREDIENTS:

½ cup butter, softened at room
    temperature
¼ cup brown sugar
½ cup sugar
1 egg
1 tsp vanilla
1¾ cups flour
1 tsp baking powder
¼ tsp salt

1. In a large mixing bowl, stir butter and sugars together with a fork. Stir in egg and vanilla. Beat well.

2. In another bowl, sift flour, baking powder, and salt together and add to butter mixture. Stir until well combined. Turn out onto counter and knead a few times until dough is smooth and soft. Add flour if sticky. Cover with plastic wrap and refrigerate at least 1 hr.

3. Using rolling pin on lightly floured surface, roll dough to ¹⁄₁₆" thickness, cut into desired shapes, arrange on baking sheets with 1" around each cookie, and bake in an oven preheated to 350°F for 8-10 minutes until edges begin to brown.

Yields **3** dozen cookies

EYE OF GOD COOKIE BOWL

I love your work! The Muralist never had it so sweet. Now, you can have your bowl of cookies and eat it too.

1. Using a small gingerbread boy cookie cutter, cut 8-12 boys from ginger cookie dough (p231) and 8-12 from vanilla cookie dough (p231). Roll cookie dough to ⅛" thickness so your finished bowl will be sturdy.

2. Arrange cookies, alternating colours, on a large deep pie pan extending their heads up the sides and overlapping their hands and feet. Press together where they overlap to make sure they adhere to each other. Bake at 350°F in a preheated oven for 10 minutes, or until lightly browned. Remove from oven and let cool 5 minutes. Gently shake pie pan to make sure cookie has not stuck to the pan then let cool completely before removing.

3. Remove cookie in one piece and decorate with royal icing (below) if desired.

ROYAL ICING

This icing dries cement-hard is great for decorating gingerbread cookies and for sticking gingerbread houses together. You can use reconstituted powdered egg whites instead of the whites of freshly cracked eggs.

INGREDIENTS:

1 egg white
1½ cups sifted icing sugar (powdered sugar)

1. Using an electric beater or a French whip, beat the egg white in a medium-sized bowl until light and frothy. Add the icing sugar and beat on low until all the icing sugar is incorporated. Increase speed to medium-high and beat until icing holds in stiff peaks when you lift out the beater. Icing should be stiff enough to hold a firm peak but soft enough to squeeze easily through a piping bag. If icing is too soft, add more sifted icing sugar. If icing is too stiff, add a few drops of cold water – a bit at a time, and beat until icing is smooth.

2. Fit a piping bag with a small round decorating tip and fill bag half-full with icing. Push icing down into bag and twist bag closed, eliminating any air pockets. Secure by wrapping with an elastic band like a ponytail. Pipe out decorations by squeezing gently on bag at the top. Set decorated cookies aside for at least 2 hours to allow the icing to harden.

AFTERWORD

Hannibal Lecter has the mind of a chef. I would know—I am a chef, too. Cooking has been my life since I was 15 years old. So I can appreciate Hannibal's attention to detail, his exacting approach to dining. I can relate to his deep appreciation for food, and to his desire to not merely please a guest, but to wow them. I can aspire to his qualities as a Renaissance man, as a sophisticated gastronomer who respects tradition and embraces science. I have always been a big Hannibal fan.

There is that little thing about cannibalism. But why so much focus on this? When Bryan Fuller walked into my Bazaar restaurant and asked me to be the Culinary Consultant for Hannibal, I never thought in terms of what a cannibal might eat. OK, maybe I got excited and started imitating Anthony Hopkins' sucking noise from the movie. But that is not the important thing. My job was to think, how can I get inside the mind of one of history's great foodies? When in life do you get the opportunity to dictate who a person is?

My role was to give Bryan and the scriptwriters some ideas about who Hannibal was when he was younger. But the one who would really be putting ideas on paper for Bryan and for the directors was Janice Poon. You see, Bryan will get an idea. He will e-mail me in the middle of the night— "José, Hannibal will be serving lamb. Any ideas?" Maybe I am in bed, maybe I am in Tokyo, but I am ready. It should be a baby lamb, the lamb of the Lord, I reply. There are so many religious overtones. Then Janice jumps in. It's crazy, but good crazy. We go back and forth, freewheeling. Anything goes. And then, Janice suggests the perfect presentation. Rack of sacrificial lamb, the ribs pointing up like a church steeple, or like praying hands. Onscreen, her work looks like a five-star meal, menacing yet delicious.

You see now how *Hannibal* is food styling unlike any other show. In only the second episode, I recommended Hannibal serve an ibérico pork loin with a Cumberland sauce and roasted, caramelized apples. Janice had to hold the loin up to her leg to make sure it truly resembled a human leg! I trust Janice completely, even with a leg of jamón ibérico de bellota, the pride of hams from Spain. Our Hannibal would know the superior quality of this Rolls Royce of ham, and he would lovingly carve it with the attention this glorious animal deserves. To this day when I watch our work come to life onscreen, I am salivating.

With the recipes in this cookbook, you will see Janice's amazing talent. You will see her beautiful drawings—the ones we discussed as a new episode evolved and changed before our eyes. They are to die for! And you will appreciate Janice's art—elevating a simple loin with a blood-red sauce, transforming a meal into a feast. You will never look at food the same way again. Enjoy.

José Andrés,
Culinary Consultant on Hannibal *and Chef/Owner of ThinkFoodGroup*

INDEX

COOKING MEASUREMENT EQUIVALENTS

The exact equivalents in the following tables have been rounded for convenience

LIQUID/DRY MEASUREMENTS

US	METRIC
¼ teaspoon	1.25 mililiters
½ teaspoon	2.5 mililiters
1 teaspoon	5 mililiters
1 tablespoon	15 mililiters
1 fluid ounce	30 mililiters
¼ cup	60 mililiters
⅓ cup	80 mililiters
½ cup	120 mililiters
1 cup	240 mililiters
1 pint	480 mililiters
1 quart	960 mililiters
1 gallon	3.84 liters
1 ounce	28 grams
1 pound	448 grams
2.2 pounds	1 kilogram

LENGTHS

US	METRIC
⅛ inch	3 milimeters
¼ inch	6 milimeters
½ inch	12 milimeters
1 inch	2.5 centimeters

OVEN TEMPERATURE

Fahrenheit	Celsius	Gas
250	120	½
275	140	1
300	150	2
325	160	3
350	180	4
375	190	5
400	200	6
425	220	7
450	230	8
475	240	9
500	260	10

Janice Poon is a world-renowned food stylist and writer. Her eclectic career in design spans magazines, wedding dresses, jewellery, sculpture and fragrances. She is an award-winning graphic novel author and currently the food stylist on the critically acclaimed NBC show, *Hannibal*, which spawned her popular behind-the-scenes blog, 'Feeding Hannibal'. Janice lives and works in Toronto, Canada.